Transnational Organized Crime

Summary of a Workshop

Committee on Law and Justice

Peter Reuter and Carol Petrie, *Editors*

Commission on Behavioral and Social Sciences and Education

National Research Council

NATIONAL ACADEMY PRESS
Washington, DC

NATIONAL ACADEMY PRESS • 2101 Constitution Avenue, N.W. • Washington, D.C. 20418

NOTICE: The project that is the subject of this report was approved by the Governing Board of the National Research Council, whose members are drawn from the councils of the National Academy of Sciences, the National Academy of Engineering, and the Institute of Medicine. The members of the committee responsible for the report were chosen for their special competences and with regard for appropriate balance.

The National Academy of Sciences is a private, nonprofit, self-perpetuating society of distinguished scholars engaged in scientific and engineering research, dedicated to the furtherance of science and technology and to their use for the general welfare. Upon the authority of the charter granted to it by the Congress in 1863, the Academy has a mandate that requires it to advise the federal government on scientific and technical matters. Dr. Bruce M. Alberts is president of the National Academy of Sciences.

The National Academy of Engineering was established in 1964, under the charter of the National Academy of Sciences, as a parallel organization of outstanding engineers. It is autonomous in its administration and in the selection of its members, sharing with the National Academy of Sciences the responsibility for advising the federal government. The National Academy of Engineering also sponsors engineering programs aimed at meeting national needs, encourages education and research, and recognizes the superior achievements of engineers. Dr. William A. Wulf is president of the National Academy of Engineering.

The Institute of Medicine was established in 1970 by the National Academy of Sciences to secure the services of eminent members of appropriate professions in the examination of policy matters pertaining to the health of the public. The Institute acts under the responsibility given to the National Academy of Sciences by its congressional charter to be an adviser to the federal government and, upon its own initiative, to identify issues of medical care, research, and education. Dr. Kenneth I. Shine is president of the Institute of Medicine.

The National Research Council was organized by the National Academy of Sciences in 1916 to associate the broad community of science and technology with the Academy's purposes of furthering knowledge and advising the federal government. Functioning in accordance with general policies determined by the Academy, the Council has become the principal operating agency of both the National Academy of Sciences and the National Academy of Engineering in providing services to the government, the public, and the scientific and engineering communities. The Council is administered jointly by both Academies and the Institute of Medicine. Dr. Bruce M. Alberts and Dr. William A. Wulf are chairman and vice chairman, respectively, of the National Research Council.

This study was supported by Contract/Grant No. 98-IJ-CX-0019 between the National Academy of Sciences and the U.S. Department of Justice. Any opinions, findings, conclusions, or recommendations expressed in this publication are those of the author(s) and do not necessarily reflect the views of the organizations or agencies that provided support for the project.

International Standard Book Number 0-309-06575-5

Additional copies of this report are available from National Academy Press, 2101 Constitution Avenue, N.W., Lockbox 285, Washington, D.C. 20055; (800) 624-6242 or (202) 334-3313 (in the Washington metropolitan area); Internet, http://www.nap.edu

Printed in the United States of America
Copyright 1999 by the National Academy of Sciences. All rights reserved.

COMMITTEE ON LAW AND JUSTICE
1998-1999

CHARLES WELLFORD (*Chair*), Center for Applied Policy Studies and the Department of Criminology and Criminal Justice, University of Maryland

JOAN PETERSILIA (*Vice Chair*), School of Social Ecology, University of California, Irvine

RUTH M. DAVIS, The Pymatuning Group, Alexandria, VA

DARNELL F. HAWKINS, African American Studies, University of Illinois at Chicago

PHILLIP B. HEYMANN, Law School and John F. Kennedy School of Government, Harvard University

CANDACE KRUTTSCHNITT, Department of Sociology, University of Minnesota

MARK LIPSEY, Department of Public Policy Studies, Vanderbilt University

COLIN LOFTIN, School of Criminal Justice, State University of New York at Albany

JOHN MONAHAN, School of Law, University of Virginia

DANIEL S. NAGIN, H. John Heinz III School of Public Policy and Management, Carnegie Mellon University

PETER REUTER, School of Public Affairs, University of Maryland

WESLEY SKOGAN, Institute for Policy Research, Northwestern University

KATE STITH, School of Law, Yale University

MICHAEL TONRY, School of Law, University of Minnesota

CATHY SPATZ WIDOM, Department of Criminal Justice & Psychology, State University of New York at Albany

CAROL PETRIE, *Study Director*
MELISSA BAMBA, *Research Associate*
KAREN AUTREY, *Senior Project Assistant*

WORKSHOP PARTICIPANTS

Peter Reuter (*Workshop Chair*), School of Public Affairs, University of Maryland
Norman Bailey, Potomac Foundation, Washington, DC
James Beachell, U.S. Central Intelligence Agency, Vienna, VA
Margaret Beare, Nathanson Center for the Study of Organized Crime and Corruption, Osgoode Hall Law School, York University
Jeffrey Berman, National Strategy Information Center, Washington, DC
Jack Blum, Lobel, Novins, and Lamont, Washington, DC
R. William Burnham, Center for Criminological Research, Oxford University
Mike DeFeo, Federal Bureau of Investigation, Washington, DC
Edgar Feige, Department of Economics, University of Wisconsin, Madison
James Finckenauer, National Institute of Justice, U.S. Department of Justice
Sally Hillsman, National Institute of Justice, U.S. Department of Justice
Eric Jeffries, National Institute of Justice, U.S. Department of Justice
Carol Kalish, Bureau of Justice Statistics, U.S. Department of Justice
Richard Langhorn, Center for Global Change & Governance, Rutgers University
Rensselear Lee, Global Advisory Services, Alexandria, VA
Frederick Martens, Claridge Casino Hotel, Atlantic City, NJ
Phyllis McDonald, National Institute of Justice, U.S. Department of Justice
William McDonald, Department of Sociology and Institute of Criminal Law, Georgetown University
Samuel McQuade, Committee on Law and Justice, National Research Council
Faith Mitchell, Division on Social and Economic Studies, National Research Council
Lois Mock, National Institute of Justice, U.S. Department of Justice
Ethan Nadelmann, Lindesmith Center, New York, NY
Tom Naylor, Department of Economics, McGill University
Nikos Passas, Department of Criminal Justice, Temple University
Raphael Perl, Congressional Research Service, Washington, DC
Carol Petrie, Committee on Law and Justice, National Research Council
Mark Sakaley, National Institute of Justice, U.S. Department of Justice

Kip Schlegel, Department of Criminal Justice, Indiana University, Bloomington
Daniel Schneider, U.S. Department of Justice, Washington, DC
Louise Shelley, Center for the Study of Transnational Organized Crime and Corruption, American University
John Sopko, U.S. Department of Commerce, Washington, DC
Sherman Teichman, Experimental College, Tufts University
Kimberley Thachuk, Institute for National Strategic Studies, National Defense University
Yonette Thomas, Committee on Law and Justice, National Research Council
Francisco Thoumi, Independent Researcher, Arlington, VA
Jeremy Travis, National Institute of Justice, U.S. Department of Justice
Elin Waring, Department of Sociology & Social Work, Lehman College
Phil Williams, Graduate School of Public and International Affairs, University of Pittsburgh
Sidney Jay Zabludoff, Independent Consultant, Washington, DC
Edwin Zedlewski, National Institute of Justice, U.S. Department of Justice

Contents

PREFACE ... ix

1 INTRODUCTION ... 1

2 DEFINITIONS AND DESCRIPTIONS ... 7
   Complexities of Definition, 7
   Describing Transnational Organized Crime, 12
   Conclusion, 20

3 MEASUREMENT ... 22
   Illegal Drugs, 22
   Other Markets, 26
   Conclusion, 27

4 ENFORCEMENT ... 28
   Need for Cooperative Relationships, 29
   Italian-American Working Group, 30
   Russia, 32
   Barriers to Cooperation, 33
   Dominance of Federal Agencies, 34
   Problems for Local Law Enforcement, 35
   Current Ad Hoc Arrangements, 37
   Conclusion, 38

5	RESEARCH AGENDA	40
	Problem Identification, 41	
	Data Sources, 46	
	Topics, 48	
	Research Methods, 51	
	Implementation Strategy, 53	

REFERENCES   54

APPENDIX: WORKSHOP AGENDA   61

Preface

Crime is becoming increasingly international. With the exception of the high homicide rates that are unique to the United States, the rates for many crimes in the developed countries of the West are quite similar and appear, at least in recent years, to rise and fall in tandem. The integration of the world's economic systems and institutions; the easing of barriers to trade, travel, and migration; and the technology that supports global communications have all increased criminal opportunities, especially across national borders, for individuals and criminal organizations worldwide. In recent years, the United States and other countries have devoted significant resources to the investigation and control of what has come to be called transnational crime.

The idea for the workshop described in this report arose out of a discussion with the research staff of the National Institute of Justice (NIJ) as the agency was developing plans for a new division, the Center for International Crime Studies. The workshop was designed to elicit ideas about the kinds of knowledge needed to understand the phenomenon of transnational crime—whether it is in fact the global threat to democracy and to free enterprise that it is sometimes portrayed to be—and to respond to it appropriately. This proved to be a difficult task, because a literature, mostly descriptive, on transnational offenses is only beginning to emerge, and the complexities of responding to it are only beginning to be understood by those responsible for its prevention and control.

NIJ made clear that they hoped the workshop participants would lay out the full scope of research issues on transnational crime rather than constraining the discussion to issues specific to NIJ's mandate to assist state and local jurisdictions. Thus the discussion covered a range of domestic and foreign policy concerns both in the United States and abroad. An issue of particular interest was whether transnational crime can in fact be measured and, if so, how to bring greater accuracy to its measurement.

The Committee on Law and Justice was fortunate in that we were able to bring together most of the best minds and scholars working on this subject. The resulting report provides useful critiques of current perspectives and makes equally useful suggestions for learning more about transnational crime. The current knowledge base in this area makes it possible at this point to map out only the most basic of research questions. And, while there was some disagreement about the nature of transnational crime problems, most workshop participants expressed their concern that these problems are of considerable political urgency and require long-term attention.

Many people made generous contributions to the workshop's success. We thank the authors of the papers presented—Louise Shelley, American University; Phillip Williams, University of Pittsburgh; Nikos Passas, Temple University; and Kip Schlegel, University of Indiana—for sharing their insights with the group. We thank the scholars who prepared comments for each of the papers—James Finkenauer, the National Institute of Justice; Elin Waring, Lehman College; Tom Naylor, McGill University; and Dan Schneider, U.S. Department of Justice.

A special thank you goes to Faith Mitchell, director of the Division on Social and Economic Studies, Commission on Behavioral and Social Sciences and Education, who guided the organization of the workshop and identified the right people as authors, discussants, and participants. We thank Christine McShane, editor, for her invaluable editorial support; and Karen Autrey, senior project assistant, for organizational assistance and logistical support. We would especially like to thank the workshop chair, Peter Reuter, University of Maryland, and Carol Petrie, director of the Committee on Law and Justice, for their work in editing this report.

This report has been reviewed in draft form by individuals chosen for their diverse perspectives and technical expertise, in accordance with procedures approved by the NRC's Report Review Committee. The purpose of this independent review is to provide candid and critical comments that will assist the institution in making the published report as sound as possible and to ensure that the report meets institutional standards for objectivity, evidence, and responsiveness to the study charge. The review comments and draft manuscript remain confidential to protect the integrity of the deliberative process.

We thank the following individuals for their participation in the review of this report: Peter Lupsha, Department of Political Science, University of New Mexico (emeritus); Mark H. Moore, John F. Kennedy School of Government, Harvard University; David Weisburd, Police Foundation, Washington, DC; Charles Wellford, Center for Applied Policy Studies, University of Maryland; and James Woolsey, Shea & Gardner, Washington, DC. Although the individuals listed above have provided constructive comments and suggestions, it must be emphasized that responsibility for the final content of this report rests entirely with the authoring committee and the institution.

Charles Wellford, *Chair*
Committee on Law and Justice

Transnational Organized Crime

1

Introduction

For the last quarter-century, Americans have become intensely conscious of the nation's vulnerability to criminal activities originating in other countries. Cocaine and heroin have caused great damage to the nation and both are produced entirely outside the United States, notwithstanding sustained efforts to suppress foreign production, inhibit smuggling, and seize traffickers' assets. Commercial and large-scale smuggling of illegal immigrants into the United States has become more prominent. Other less well-articulated criminal threats to national sovereignty (such as the smuggling of chlorofluorocarbons and the killing of a journalist in the United States, in reprisal for investigative reporting on drug traffickers in Columbia) have prominence from time to time. Western European governments have also become concerned with these problems.

This phenomenon of transnational crime has been affected by three related factors. First is the globalization of the economy, which brings U.S. citizens and corporations into increasing contact with foreign entities. In particular, there is unease about the potential ability of foreigners to manipulate funds for criminal purposes within the United States. The end of the cold war has contributed, in a number of ways, to this economic integration and the growth of opportunities for illicit transactions across borders (Winer, 1997b). Second is the rise in the numbers and the heterogeneity of immigrants. Although famously and self-consciously a nation of immigrants, the United States has never had such large numbers of people arrive from places so scattered around the world, bringing with them social and commercial networks that make law enforcement more difficult and that facilitate conspiracy. The porousness of the border with Mexico, which has only recently become a major trading partner for the United States, in particular reinforces people's perception that the nation is not in control of its destiny. Third, improved communications technology makes borders even more permeable, but by inconspicuous means. Criminal activities can be carried out in the United States by foreigners without anyone's crossing a border (Marx, 1998).

No doubt one can find historical precedents for all of these factors or even a period in time when all three of them appeared as important parts of the American reality. But they are very prominent now and it takes only a small number of incidents, such as the extensive frauds committed by the Bank of Commerce and Credit International (BCCI) or the capturing of a large group of Chinese immigrants being smuggled in a ship, to give substance to general fears.

Transnational organized crime has attracted a good deal of media attention; the activities of criminal organizations tend to make good stories. Politically there has also been some highly visible activity, with President Clinton devoting two major United Nations speeches to these matters and promulgating a Presidential Decision Directive (Number 42, October 22, 1995) against international organized crime. In the 1995 meeting of the Group of Seven (G7) nations, control of transnational organized crime was a principal item on the agenda. At the programmatic level, the U.S. government has become involved in efforts to help other governments (e.g., Colombia, Italy, and Russia) deal with criminal organizations that pose a threat to both the United States and the host nation. Systematic research on these problems, however, has lagged considerably.

During the 1990s, the National Institute of Justice (NIJ) of the U.S. Department of Justice became interested in international crime problems and the ways in which they affect domestic crime in the United States. NIJ recently has strengthened its links with the international community in important ways: through membership in a worldwide network of criminological institutes affiliated with the United Nations (UN); through its participation in the development of the United Nations Criminal Justice Information Network; through initiation of the United Nations Online Justice Clearinghouse, an Internet-based system electronically linking the institutes to the UN network; and by establishing a new International Center within NIJ. In addition to building links with criminal justice researchers in other nations, these activities have enabled the United States to gain better access to internationally available research information on transnational organized crime. Most international research efforts are descriptive rather than analytical, however.

It is against this backdrop that, in 1997, the National Institute of Justice asked the National Research Council's Committee on Law and Justice to organize a workshop on transnational organized crime. NIJ was interested in exploring ways in which to promote U.S. research interests and to augment the UN's research activities with regard to these problems. Research interest in the United States has been stimulated by the difficulty of controlling the high volume of trafficking in illicit drugs, illegal immigrants, and other illegal goods and services. Reports of high profits from these activities have also generated concern that significant flows of illegal cash may pose a threat to the integrity of financial structures in this country and others.

Many questions focus on what is intrinsically new about these crimes and what kinds of knowledge are needed to prevent and control them. Use of traditional investigative methods, such as intelligence gathering and the use of informants, appears inadequate to the task. The overarching purpose of the workshop was to determine whether transnational crime is a persistent and measurable phenomenon that merits its own research attention, and whether an agenda for systematic domestic and international research on it could be developed. The workshop was designed with four specific goals:

1. To explore alternative ways of defining and conceptualizing transnational organized crime;

2. To assess the ability to measure transnational organized crime, focusing on the extent and distribution of perceived or real increases in criminal activities and the power of the organizations involved;

3. To identify possible enforcement and control responses to transnational crime problems, especially as they are manifest at the state and local level; and

4. To examine the factors that facilitate the function, organization, and structural patterns of transnational crime so that prevention approaches could be designed in collaboration with legitimate enterprises and international partners.

The Committee on Law and Justice was responsible for developing this two-day workshop, held June 17 and 18, 1998, in Washington, D.C. The participants represented a range of disciplines, including economics, sociology, psychology, law, foreign affairs, public policy, and other professions; they also included federal officials and law enforcement personnel. A number of papers were commissioned in advance to pull together research findings reflecting the workshop's goals. A focused discussion was conducted on measurement issues. Through the presentations of the papers and interactive discussions, which provide the structure for this report, the participants:

- Distilled the descriptive research with regard to the definition, scope, and organization of transnational organized crime and discussed the limitations of that research (Chapter 2).
- Explored measurement issues, particularly the extent to which they are intertwined with problems of definition and the attendant difficulties that are associated with conducting systematic research in this area (Chapter 3).
- Examined enforcement practices and problems, emphasizing the dominance of federal agencies, the need for bilateral or multilateral cooperative efforts, and the lack of awareness and expertise at the local level, where much transnational crime first surfaces (Chapter 4).
- Considered promising directions for future research on transnational organized crime, with emphasis on laying a foundation for the development of future prevention and control strategies (Chapter 5).

The agenda was concerned with U.S. policy issues and the various ways in which the United States should be dealing with these offenses. Transnational organized crime activities taking place entirely in other nations were also considered specifically in terms of U.S. interests. We also used instances of organized crime activities taking place in other nations for illustrative purposes and for developing insights about the practical challenge of improving operational effectiveness and research approaches. An emphasis was placed on activities in two countries, Mexico and Russia, that were considered particularly important because their organized crime problems have significant domestic and foreign policy consequences for the United States.

Four prominent scholars agreed to write papers, which served as focal points for discussion. The papers have been bound as workshop products for submission to the sponsor and other workshop participants. The authors are expected to submit them for publication to journals or other dissemination organs.

This report attempts to capture the richness of the many insights and impressions offered at the workshop. The participants' perspectives on the issues and appropriate research approaches varied widely. Keenly aware of the political controversy that surrounds many of these issues, they understood that shifts in the political or legal environment—for example, legislative changes that criminalize once-legal behavior or decriminalize formerly illegal activity—can complicate the conduct of research on these matters, counterbalancing even the best research designs or measurement systems.

As can be seen throughout this volume, and particularly in the chapter on definitions, considerable difficulty characterized the framing of the workshop; it is therefore important to clarify what is and is not included here, and why. For example, a decision was made to deemphasize terrorism and to focus on other types of transnational crime. There were several reasons for this. First, terrorism receives a good deal of attention in these kinds of gatherings and tends to overwhelm other crime types, which may seem far less serious in comparison. Second, terrorism differs from other transnational crimes, for example in its clients or consumers and in the way terrorist acts (whether domestic or international) versus other crimes are addressed in the operational and academic worlds. It seemed a better idea to develop some specificity in one area before attempting to put them together, and a workshop seemed ideally suited for this. Third, many transnational crime problems unrelated to terrorism are arising in Western Europe and in the emerging democracies of Eastern Europe, and these crimes are having both direct and indirect effects in the United States. These crime problems also are of interest because of their impact on new law enforcement infrastructures being developed in these countries.

That said, however, it was impossible to exclude from this report all discussion of terrorism, and the national security apparatuses that deal with it. Indeed, one workshop participant made the point that there is no consensus about the nature of transnational threats in the national security community, nor is there much discrimination between terrorism and other kinds of transnational offenses. Thus, it is important to acknowledge that terrorism is included in the UN definition of transnational crime, and (along with drug trafficking) is the crime most worrisome to the public. Moreover, terrorism may be importantly connected to other kinds of transnational crime, either because some criminal groups are enlisted in terrorist acts, or terrorists themselves act for pecuniary as well as political motives, or because some terrorist groups use criminal means to achieve their nonmonetary aims. These dangers are nowhere more evident than in the trafficking of nuclear weapons, which is mentioned in relation to Russian organized crime in Chapters 4 and 5.

A second issue involving the goals of the workshop is whether and how a definition of transnational organized crime can be developed for research purposes. During the course of the workshop discussions, it became clear that no single definition has currency or agreement. In general, the workshop participants agreed that the field is not ready for a single perspective and were content to let 1,000 flowers (definitions and concepts) bloom. In addition, as the discussion of measurement illustrates, deriving a research definition was constrained by the fact that, with the exception of drug trafficking, there are no major datasets on transnational crime, such as survey or longitudinal data, and virtually no data sources independent of operations. At the current stage of research development, data can come only from investigations or litigation, and through case studies and observational studies. Thus, while the workshop focused specifically on research issues, the entire discussion and especially the research agenda outlined in Chapter 5 should be considered in the context of the need for operations and research to work hand in glove, at least for a while.

The Committee on Law and Justice hopes that this report will be a stimulus to more thorough and ongoing consideration of the research needs in this policy area.

2

Definitions and Descriptions

Definitions can be developed in at least two ways: either inductively, by observing how a word or term is used, or deductively, by translating a highly abstract concept into something more usable for description, measurement, or control. A single definition may not serve all purposes equally well. We give more emphasis in this report to definitions suitable for research than for enforcement, although we recognize that, especially in a field driven by policy and operational concerns, the development of a scientific nomenclature often depends on terms and definitions used in practice.

COMPLEXITIES OF DEFINITION

The term "transnational crime" was developed by the United Nations (UN) Crime and Criminal Justice Branch in 1974 to guide discussion at one of the quinquennial UN crime conferences. As described by Mueller (1998), it was a criminological term, with no claim to providing a juridical concept, and consisted simply of a list of five activities: (1) crime as business: organized crime, white-collar crime, and corruption; (2) offenses involving works of art and other cultural property; (3) criminality associated with alcoholism and drug abuse (especially illicit traffic); (4) violence of transnational and comparative international significance; and (5) criminality associated with migration and flight from natural disasters and hostilities. Twenty years later, a single-sentence conceptual definition was added by the UN: "offenses whose inception, prevention and/or direct effect or indirect effects involved more than one country" (United Nations, 1995). This definition may have use for an international organization, in terms of defining jurisdiction for its programs or treaties, but is less useful for measurement. The list of offense categories was at the same time expanded to 18, to include such varied activities as trade in human body parts, environmental crimes, and fraudulent bankruptcies. The transnational element of some of these categories seems somewhat strained; for example, it includes all computer crimes because computers are now linked across national boundaries, although a specific computer crime may involve no party or transaction outside the United States.

One possible conceptual definition was offered at the workshop: "acts that are offenses in one state that involve actions or actors in another state, requiring more than a single opportunistic transaction between individuals." The first part of the definition elides the question of whether both jurisdictions criminalize the same activities, and the second makes the distinction between transnational organized crime and the broader phenomenon of transnational crime.

In a world with great disparities in the detail and reach of the code of criminal law, legal definitions of "offense" may be too narrow conceptually. Many nations have been created in the past 10 years; some still have weak systems of written laws. One participant at the workshop suggested that the definition be expanded to include "acts that entail avoidable and unnecessary harm to society, which are serious enough to warrant state intervention, and similar to other kinds of acts criminalized in some countries."

It is not clear how important the qualifier "organized" is for the definition. Precisely because it involves criminal activities that cross national boundaries, some degree of organization is usually required, generally a considerable amount. Certainly, as Phillip Williams notes in his workshop paper, some very serious cross-border crimes can be individual. For example, a toxic waste hauler in San Diego who dumps into border waters, thus creating pollution or toxic hazards in Mexico, is probably committing a transnational crime but on an individual basis, with no transnational collaborator. Moreover, these kinds of acts present legal authorities with distinctive problems; for example, gathering evidence in Mexico so as to permit a prosecution under U.S. environmental law may be difficult.

The workshop, and most of the research literature, suggest that the main action involves organizations. But the organization of crime is very different from organized crime. Ko-lin Chin, having studied Chinese criminal gangs and their many activities, concludes that "human smuggling is not organized crime but rather it is crime that is organized.... It is a trade that needs organized participation and execution but it does not appear to be linked with traditional organized crime groups" (Chin, 1998).

The definitions developed in the organized crime research field (Maltz, 1994; see also Jacobs and Panterella, 1998) do not seem particularly relevant for transnational organized crime, although some individual characteristics may apply. Maltz's list of organized crime characteristics (the definition is descriptive rather than deductive) includes: corruption, violence, sophistication, continuity, structure, discipline, ideology (or lack thereof), multiple enterprises, and involvement in legitimate enterprises. These may reasonably be described as the common features of the American Mafia and some other ethnically centered American criminal groups of the first three quarters of this century, many of them building control of specific local illegal markets through their control of corrupt police departments and political machines (see, e.g., Haller, 1994).

The emphasis on the use of violence and corruption to control markets, however, does not seem central to transnational organized crime. The usual incentives for violence in organized crime (discipline of subordinates, succession to leadership, transactional integrity, territorial protection) are attenuated when organizations are not highly centralized and the notion of territoriality is strained. Territories are associated with localness; transnational organized crime entities aspire to broader reach than that. Suborning rangers in African game parks to obtain protected species of animals or plants may be an important element of the international trade in those species, but it can be done indirectly or can be avoided by the smuggling organization if it merely encourages local poachers to seek out the desired objects. Although it is no doubt useful to obtain cooperation from U.S. border personnel for importing illegal aliens, the paucity of cases in the face of a persistent investigative effort suggests that smugglers mostly succeed without that cooperation.

This is not to claim that transnational organized crime generates neither violence nor corruption. In particular, the drug trades at the import level are associated with both violence and corruption in some major producer and transshipment nations. But both evidence and argument suggest that these phenomena do not revolve around the control of activities or markets, as is the case for organized crime domestically.

The other characteristics listed by Maltz are secondary for American organized crime and seem even more so for the transnational variety. Sophistication may help in complex financial crimes, but much smuggling is quite simple, both operationally and organizationally. Similarly, a stolen car exporting ring may engage in no other criminal activity but still involve transnational criminal activity with a substantial organizational superstructure.

Indeed, Williams (1998) has argued persuasively that the organized crime literature has been too focused on concepts of either markets or centralized organizations, when there has been a shift, in both legitimate businesses and illicit enterprises (and even some terrorist groups), to the use of networks. Recent work by Finckenauer and Waring (1998) on Russian organized crime (more correctly, criminal activities by Russian émigrés) conforms more to the network notion. Networks represent relations among criminal actors that allow them to collaborate opportunistically with other members most appropriate to the specific opportunity presented. This may be particularly useful for understanding the emergence and functioning of transnational organized crime. The network is likely to have a core group of people who are fairly tightly connected and then a more dispersed set of participants, most of whom will collaborate only in response to initiative by the core group and who have more specialized functions. Other characteristics of offenders or offending groups may be important to the definition as well. We have learned even in street crime that it makes sense to look at offenders as well as the offense; this is the whole idea of "dangerous offenders." It is important practically, because high-rate offenders commit many of the offenses. It is important in justice terms, because sustained offending seems morally more culpable than one-time offending. The latter is particularly pertinent to the notion of offenders engaged in ongoing criminal enterprises.

Several participants noted that for purposes of research, definition is necessarily entangled with measurement (treated in Chapter 3). That points to a definition built around well-defined activities; for example, one might focus on how many tons of chlorofluorocarbons (CFCs) were imported illicitly into the United States from countries that were exempted under the international protocol signed in Montreal in 1987 (perhaps through analysis of reported sales of CFCs and recorded legitimate imports) and how many persons/businesses were engaged in this smuggling. But some activities that might be included present greater challenges to definition through measurement. For example, the UN list includes insurance fraud, presumably limited to those instances in which there is some involvement of persons/entities outside the host country. However, insurers have incentives to conceal that they have been defrauded. Given that most of these offenses remain unsolved, it is highly unlikely that an estimate of the transnational organized crime component of insurance fraud can be generated.

Transnational organized crime is also close to transnational white-collar crime. Legitimate corporations making bribery payments to foreign officials for facilitating the smuggling of their products into nations that have prohibited them are certainly elements of what is referred to as transnational organized crime by some researchers (e.g., Passas, 1996). Transnational white-collar crime is likely to fit any of the abstract definitions offered for transnational organized crime; a question is whether they are sufficiently different in their sources and adverse consequences that including white-collar activities makes an already complex topic intractable.

A sense of the fragility of the definition can be garnered by noting that the extent of transnational crime is influenced simply by the number of nations and their size. The breakup of the Soviet Union into 15 separate states means that many offenses, such as Georgians selling untaxed liquor in Moscow, have now become transnational. Bovenkirk (1998) has noted that the European Union, comparable to the United States in population, area, and total economic activity, involves 15 national sovereignties. Thus whereas a California swindle of a New York insurance company is simply a white-collar crime, the European equivalent, a British swindle of a Greek insurer, would be transnational.

In deriving a definition for research (or operational) purposes, some attention should be given to a listing of the principal activities involved and describing actual or hypothetical cases. The following list is a starting point, covering only activities that seem to be significant at the turn of the twenty-first century:

- **Smuggling**
  - Commodities
  - Drugs
  - Protected species
- Contraband (goods subject to tariffs or quotas)
  - Stolen cars
  - Tobacco products

- Services
  - Immigrants
  - Prostitution
  - Indentured servitude
  - Money laundering
  - Fraud

It has been noted that, in all social science research, definition is very much a matter of social construction; the choice of definition is just that, a choice, and is not dictated by some external reality. A variety of abstract definitions can reasonably compete here, but a listing of activities should also be useful for defining the current field of research.

DESCRIBING TRANSNATIONAL ORGANIZED CRIME

The United Nation's categories of transnational crime include traditional international crimes such as hijacking and terrorism; various types of frauds; trafficking in stolen goods or illicit commodities, such as weapons and human beings; and environmental crime. The latter three, which share a common motivation, namely the desire for illicit profits, were the main focus of the workshop. As a starting point, participants were concerned with the impact of these crimes in the United States, which serves not only as a lucrative market for illicit goods and services but also as a supplier of some commodities or services for other countries. Transnational crime groups import illegal drugs and other expensive commodities into the United States, and also export such stolen goods as arms, tobacco products, and cars to consumers in other countries. Furthermore, as the world's largest economy and as a major international money center, the United States provides the financial institutions through which the profits of transnational crime activities flow. Elaborate schemes to defraud financial institutions and businesses occur in the United States as well as many other countries.

Workshop participants were mindful, however, that what organized crime does abroad has an impact on U.S. foreign policy interests. Americans are concerned about organized crime in Mexico, for example, not only because drugs come into the United States from that country, but also because of the influence of organized crime on the Mexican government, and its implications for the U.S. foreign policy interests there. The following brief examples provide some insight into the operations of transnational crime groups.

Auto Theft Rings

Many stolen vehicles exported to foreign countries originate in the United States. These crimes are easily executed and can even be perpetrated by single individuals attempting to defraud their insurance companies. But more often, theft export rings, operating out of immigrant communities throughout the United States, are responding to the demand for these vehicles from contacts in their home countries. Some of these crimes are simple theft and export operations, but others involve sophisticated counterfeiting techniques and network operations. Stolen cars are fitted with counterfeit vehicle identification number (VIN) markings and license plates, taken to ports, crated and sealed in intentionally mislabeled containers, and shipped overseas (National Insurance Crime Bureau, 1999).

In one case, a large, loosely organized, but very proficient group in Florida was found to have been smuggling stolen vehicles with expertly counterfeited VINs to countries in South America. The group had ties to an employee at the Port of Miami who was selling lists of VINS from previously exported vehicles. A special investigative task force uncovered this auto theft ring when they found some of these counterfeit VINS on several recovered stolen vehicles that had been "renumbered" by the group for sale in the United States.

Even though some manufacturers embed covert antitheft, security features in their VIN labels, it is almost impossible to identify or recover most exported stolen vehicles. Many foreign countries cannot identify stolen vehicles because they have no VIN standards or requirements, component part markings, registration and title files, or manufacturing and shipping records. It is important, however, not to overstate the magnitude of auto theft as a transnational crime problem in the United States. Two-thirds of the 1.4 million autos stolen annually in this country are recovered (National Insurance Crime Bureau, 1999). Some unknown proportion of the remainder winds up in so-called chop shops—usually in the United States, but sometimes in Mexican border towns—where stolen vehicles are stripped and their parts and accessories sold separately; the rest are assumed to have been exported for resale in other countries.

Smuggling of Aliens

Shelley (1998) has noted that human beings are trafficked for a number of purposes: prostitution, cheap labor, and taking up illegal residence in the country of destination. The Immigration and Naturalization Service estimates that about 275,000 illegal immigrants enter the United States in a given year, and that, in 1997, about 5 million illegal immigrants had become "permanent" residents (Immigration and Naturalization Service, 1999).[1] Most, at least from Mexico, probably do not pay professionals for services in getting across the border safely. The few studies of trafficking in illegal immigrants have focused primarily on Asia and Mexico but, overall, little has been done to examine the effects on the United States of trafficking in illegal aliens from these areas or from other countries of the Caribbean and the former Soviet Union (Shelley, 1998; Winer, 1997a).

Trafficking in human beings differs from other types of smuggling in that the individual often must repay the trafficker after arriving at his or her destination. Most smugglers or criminal organizations relinquish control of an illicit item once it is delivered, but traffickers frequently maintain control of illegal immigrants, forcing them to work for low wages and to commit crimes to support themselves (Shelley, 1998). Conditions of transit often endanger the lives of the people being trafficked. Moreover, when families or individuals are unable to pay the large sums charged for illegal transit, the trafficked individual may be violently assaulted, raped, or sometimes murdered (Chin, 1997).

A noteworthy form of this crime involves illegal trafficking in women and girls, which is characterized by certain patterns no matter where it occurs. Typically, a woman or girl is recruited in her home country by an agent, who promises a good job in another country, but instead forces her, through debt bondage, into prostitution. The offer of a job is sometimes accompanied by a payment to the woman's family at the time of recruitment, a debt she must repay with interest. The debt increases because of charges for her transportation—which usually are enormous because of the need to avoid detection—and for food, clothes, medicine, and lodging provided by the waiting brothel owner or pimp (Caldwell and Galster, 1997; International Organization for Migration, 1997).

---

[1] The 275,000 represents the net addition to the stock of illegal immigrants each year. Many millions may cross the border in both directions; some are here only briefly and others return to their home country only briefly.

Escape is virtually impossible without repaying these debts, which are often between $25,000 and $30,000 (Shelley, 1998; Chin, 1997). Leaving the brothel without repayment invites retribution against the woman and frequently against her parents or other family members. The risk of arrest on immigration charges also keeps the woman dependent on the brothel owner or pimp, as do other factors, such as the distance from home, lack of familiarity with the local language, and consequent inability to find local support networks.

Although most frequently described as a problem in Asian and certain European countries, enforced prostitution of immigrant women and girls also has been found to occur in the United States (Dombrink and Song, 1992; Chin, 1997). Other immigrants pay to be smuggled into the United States to flee poverty or persecution, and they also experience debt bondage. In addition to transportation, smugglers charge exorbitant rents for substandard, abandoned, or even condemned housing. Some immigrants end up in prostitution, and others are forced to work in sweatshops, sell drugs, or become traffickers themselves to pay off their debt.

Financial Crimes

Financial crimes—bank and insurance fraud and money laundering—committed by transnational crime groups are among the most complex and difficult to detect. Many frauds are large in scale and use international telecommunications technology to quickly move illicit profits out of the country where the offense occurs. Passas (1993) has asserted that "if money is the lifeblood of criminal enterprises, banks are the veins through which it flows." Bank frauds are troublesome for investigators because banks avoid accountability by hiding behind veils of confidentiality and complex organizational systems. Even serious misconduct is handled with great discretion, usually settled in a way that avoids costly and prolonged litigation, and without either admitting or denying guilt. Many such frauds are perpetrated with the witting (or unwitting) collusion of high-level corporate officials or mid- to high-level government officials. Some are carrying out authorized policies, and some are simply personally corrupt.

Sparrow (1999) has recently found that health care fraud remains at alarmingly high levels, despite attention from law enforcement, and that major scams are artfully designed to circumvent routine controls and remain invisible for long periods. Russian émigré crime groups have been particularly active in insurance fraud schemes victimizing Medicare and other health insurance providers in the United States. In the most costly of these crimes ever prosecuted, mobile health clinics were established to defraud Medicare and Medicaid. "Patients were lured to clinics or sites serviced by mobile vans for [fake] comprehensive physical examinations, with bogus claims of 'state-of-the-art' testing offered 'free of charge' or at a nominal cost to the patient" (U.S. Senate, 1996). These phony medical clinics then submitted claims for these examinations and tests to insurers. Losses to the U.S. Treasury and private health companies totaled around $1 billion and forced the state of California to completely restructure its public health insurance programs (Raine and Cilluffo, 1994). Shelley has noted that, after seven years of investigation, law enforcement agencies were able to recover only a small amount of the money because it was laundered outside the country, virtually as the claim payments came in. This is also an example of a crime that was organized, rather than of organized crime; that is, two individuals rather than an organized group perpetrated this particular fraud (Finkenauer and Waring, 1998). Investigations have also identified similar schemes in which Russian crime groups in the United States staged car accidents and then established phony medical clinics for the purpose of submitting fraudulent claims for unnecessary treatments.

Nexus Between Legal and Illegal Activities

By their very nature, many transnational criminal activities, especially financial crimes, require the tacit or open cooperation of legitimate organizations and actors. In the abstract, organizations could be perceived as either legitimate groups that commit no crime or as criminal groups with purely criminal purposes. In the real world, however, the activities of many organizations, both legitimate and criminal, fall between these extremes.

Transnational crimes sometimes are committed by criminal organizations in pursuit of criminal goals and sometimes by legitimate organizations in the pursuit of otherwise legal business goals. The illegal drug trade has tints of both. The smuggling and marketing of illegal commodities for profit reflects the purely illicit organization, and the laundering of the resulting funds by financial institutions represents the tacit participation of the legitimate one. The corruption through extortion or bribery of public officials in a country in order to do business within their borders is a common example of the reverse: legitimate ends accomplished with criminal means. One workshop participant noted that when doing business in countries with weak governments where contracts cannot be enforced, all organizations break some laws.

A specific example of linkages between the legitimate and the illegitimate is the Bank of Credit and Commerce International (BCCI) scandal. Passas (1996) has detailed the web of relationships between the BCCI and corporate leaders, political figures, and other prominent government officials and world leaders in most of the 72 countries where the bank operated. Its capitalization by the ruler of Abu Dhabi and the Bank of America in 1972 gave the bank the credibility to grow quickly and the cachet to establish these relationships. It was able to obtain deposits, open new branches, gain preferential treatment, handle a country's U.S. commodity credits, and gain respectability (Passas, 1996). Many individuals and organizations profited from the bank's operations.

Despite these advantages, the bank was insolvent from the beginning. Its top managers manipulated the bank's accounts to conceal losses, keep deposits off the books, hide illegal investments in U.S. financial institutions, and generate false profits (Passas, 1996). Illegal or, at the very least, poor banking practices made these problems worse. For example, a loan to the Gulf Group of shipping companies was larger than the bank's capital base, and the loan was not serviced, resulting in unsustainable losses of over $1 billion in the 1980s. Passas notes that the liquidators could not account for several billion dollars, and subsequent investigations into BCCI's practices, as well as press reports, fueled a massive international scandal. The bank, ostensibly established to serve the poor and poor countries, was accused instead of serving Colombian drug barons, a number of intelligence agencies, several prominent Third World dictators, money launderers, arms traders, and tax evaders, among others (Passas, 1996). It is still not altogether clear whether the intent was criminal from the outset, or whether this was a legitimate enterprise run amok.

By the mid-1980s, auditors and regulators had detected these illegal practices. Directors and shareholders also were aware of BCCI's heavy losses and other problems. Yet, in several instances, powerful actors lobbied openly or behind the scenes on behalf of BCCI, trying to convince the authorities that the rumors and evidence about BCCI were baseless (Passas, 1996). Most of these individuals, later implicated in the BCCI scandal, claimed that they were deceived and were unaware of unlawful practices, despite many warning signs (Singapore did not allow BCCI to operate there, and Great Britain and the United States placed severe restrictions on its operations). The most benign interpretation is that they were indeed fooled. Passas concluded that the system in place to detect and control such abuses functions so badly that they may be more frequent than is realized.

This nexus in the banking world between the legitimate and illegitimate—essentially the connection between corruption and money—goes to the heart of concerns about transnational crime threats. For example, neither small crime networks nor criminal cartels could launder or hide their illegal profits without banking safe havens. The United States, the G7 nations, and the World Bank have been trying to combat money laundering since the late 1980s. Despite their efforts, the U.S. Department of the Treasury has had to issue advisories calling for enhanced scrutiny of certain transactions from banks in Mexico, and all transactions originating from the Seychelles (in the Indian Ocean), and Barbuda and Antigua, a small island nation in the the Caribbean (Financial Crimes Enforcement Network, 1996a, 1996b, 1996c, 1999). The activities of these havens strengthen the influence of what Anthony Lake, President Clinton's national security adviser, has called international criminal conglomerates and constitute a potential threat to the global banking community. U.S. institutions and the public also may be contributing to this problem. The Federal Reserve fined one well-regarded American bank $950,000 for its compromised behavior involving money-laundering by officials at one of its branches in Beverly Hills, California, in 1993 (Lupsha, 1995). And, according to one workshop participant, the U.S. General Accounting Office estimates compliance with the requirement to report income kept in foreign banks at only 8 percent. The president has called on the international community to come together in a common cause against these activities, to work with other nations to outlaw these activities, and to consider sanctions against recalcitrant nations (Lake, 1998).

Transnational crime produces benefits for some people, giving corporations and governments an incentive to develop relationships with organized criminal groups, or at least tolerate their activities. Historically, the smuggling of American cigarettes into highly protected markets resulted in the crumbling of resistance to foreign smoking products in those markets and in increased profits for American tobacco companies. Direct harm to the United States from cigarette smuggling may have been minimal, except for the smuggling capacities that were created to perhaps serve other illegal markets. Illegal drugs are also illustrative. Several workshop participants pointed out that the drug trade does not *just* cause harm. In some poor countries, it generates employment, income, and foreign exchange, provides a better standard of living for hundreds of thousands of farmers in the countryside, and produces capital for legitimate investment.

In South America, organized crime in many regions is a major source of funding for political campaigns. As one workshop participant noted, "It pays for the buses, the barbecues, the chicken dinners. It gets out the vote." In Colombia and Peru, the proceeds from organized crime may provide a kind of bulwark against spreading insurgent movements by funding counterinsurgency and paramilitary organizations that cooperate with the countries' military. Aggressive enforcement, such as the busting of drug cartels, in these areas may simply lead to a takeover of the illicit activities by the insurgents, rather than to their eradication.

Historical Perspective

Some authors maintain that there is little new to the phenomenon of transnational organized crime. Tom Naylor argued at the workshop that the smuggling of highly taxed tea into Britain in the 18th century was a large-scale transnational organized crime activity, even involving corruption on the part of governments and legitimate corporations. The opium wars of the 19th century were initiated by a government-sanctioned cartel, the British East India Company, seeking to expand its market against the wishes and laws of the Chinese government. The Japanese government in the period between World War I and II was a principal supplier in the illegal cocaine market, developing coca fields in Formosa for that purpose (Karch, 1998). Rent seeking (i.e., the expectation of extra earnings through gifts or favors) by officials is a long-standing phenomenon, and organizations with international ambitions often have the capability to manipulate that behavior. In recent years, according to this school of thought, all that has changed is the scale, although adherents concede that scale matters.

Ethnicity and Transnational Crime

Ethnic minorities, particularly those newly arrived in a country, turn out to have an especially important role in transnational organized crime, in both the United States and other rich countries. Bovenkirk (1998) gives examples: Vietnamese gangsters have tended to dominate cigarette smuggling in Berlin; prostitution in London has long been heavily influenced by a small number of Maltese; and foreign and immigrant criminal groups were shown to be the principal figures in organized crime in the Netherlands (Fijnhaut et al., 1997).

The United States has a long history of such involvement by new ethnic minorities; the Irish were conspicuous among the urban racketeers in the late 19th century, mostly providing illegal gambling services, and Italians and Eastern Europeans were prominent in the bootlegging industry of the 1920s (Haller, 1977). The difference is that these gangs made little use of their roots in another country. Even though bootleggers imported a large share of the illegal alcohol sold during Prohibition, their connections to Europe were irrelevant for that activity. Only the early Mafia control of the heroin-importing industry depended on their ability to work with gangs in Sicily and Corsica (Cressey, 1969).

Today ethnic groups involved in criminal activities appear to make much more extensive use of their foreign connections. One factor that has led Colombia to become the center of the cocaine production industry is the strength of its ties to a large immigrant community in the United States, which was established well before the drug trade was significant. By 1990 the census reported that 286,000 U.S. residents were born in Colombia, about twice as many U.S. residents as were born in Bolivia or Peru (Bureau of the Census, 1993).

Theories to explain the connection between minority or immigrant status and criminal activity are not hard to find (Tonry, 1997). Such groups have a comparative advantage in smuggling and domestic distribution of goods and services from their home country; better connections with the producers and corrupt authorities there; and a protective immigrant community that is not yet trusting of local authorities, thus providing barriers to the recruitment of effective informants or the conduct of investigations generally. Furthermore, these groups are often denied opportunity within the legitimate economy, whether because of limited proficiency in the host country language, poor education, or discrimination by employers. The strength of kinship networks in these communities also facilitates the development of trust, which is an important factor in criminal enterprise.

CONCLUSION

Arriving at a single definition that usefully limits the field of research but also covers the full range of issues and problems described here proved very difficult. Clearly the definition, at least initially, must be based on the laws of the United States, other countries, or international law. The crimes on the UN list provide an interesting starting point. Many involve the production and distribution of goods and services that are prohibited by one or more of these bodies of law. Motivation—committing illegal acts for money or a cause—is important to the definition. The definition must also take into account the nature of the offenders and the level and type of organization required to commit the crime. Harm, both level and type, is critical to defining transnational crime problems. Just as operational agencies allocate their investigative resources to what they see as the most important cases, researchers may want to reserve the designation of transnational organized crime to mean certain offenses carried out by certain kinds of organizations—i.e., above some threshold of size, durability, capacity, or harm. Developing a variety of definitions that include some or all of these elements and are based in law enforcement and other justice system responses may be one path to sorting through these problems of nomenclature. Fleshing out the description in an analytically coherent manner may provide another path to better research.

3

Measurement

The phenomenon of transnational organized crime is real. Therefore, once definitional issues are settled, it must be susceptible to measurement, although formidable conceptual and institutional barriers remain, even using a definition that is principally a list of activities, or one that is closely allied with operational definitions. Moreover, as Edgar Feige noted at the workshop, measurement is often the single most important way of focusing attention on the definitional issue; measurement requires conceptual clarity.

This chapter briefly describes efforts to measure various aspects of transnational organized crime to date, identifying the sources of information and analytic techniques used. The discussion of research directions in Chapter 5 builds on this.

ILLEGAL DRUGS

By far the best explored of transnational illegal markets is that for drugs. The most recent estimates, those for 1995, give a total of about $60 billion in retail sales in the United States, the largest component being cocaine ($30 billion). Illicit drug expenditures equal about 1.5 percent of legitimate personal consumption expenditures in the United States. These estimates are the result of well-documented and sophisticated calculations sponsored by the Office of National Drug Control Policy (ONDCP) (e.g.,

1997). Notwithstanding the carefulness of these calculations, which integrate numerous data sources, there remains very considerable uncertainty, as indicated by 25 percent adjustments between 1995 and 1997, in the totals for specific years (compare Office of National Drug Control Policy, 1995, 1997). We start by examining the consumption-based estimates, which are regarded as the stronger.

They are of particular interest because of the richness and scale of the available data. The estimates build on a variety of datasets (primarily the National Household Survey on Drug Abuse and the Drug Use Forecasting system, now called Arrestee Drug Abuse Monitoring) to develop estimates of the number of people using each type of drug, categorized into two groups by intensity of use (heavy, occasional) and the dollars they spend. Total consumption is then deduced by dividing total expenditures by prices,[1] derived from a series maintained by the Drug Enforcement Agency (DEA). This apparently backward method of deducing quantity consumed from expenditure reflects the fact that drug users do not directly observe the quantity purchased and can thus only report expenditures. For example, a heroin user may spend $20 on two "dime bags," each of which contains white powder that he or she believes weighs 20 milligrams, including 10 milligrams of heroin. Analysis of actual purchases shows enormous variability in what is actually contained in such a bag (e.g., Weatherburn and Lind, 1997).

The estimate includes no adjustment for underreporting in expenditures by survey respondents, although in other expenditure surveys the totals produced for legal items are substantially less than what is known from other sources to be spent on the category of items. For example, for alcohol it is difficult to produce, from self-report surveys, an estimate even two-thirds as large as expenditures shown by tax records. Manning and colleagues (1991), in a recent and sophisticated analysis of the National Health Interview Survey responses, estimate that they were able to account for only half of actual total alcohol consumption.[2]

---

[1]Caulkins (1995) notes that the price referred to in these calculations is a "reference" price, based on a standardized purchase of 1 pure gram and that this may not reflect the average price actually paid if there is a change in the size composition of purchases.

[2]The underestimation may be the consequence of many factors: an incomplete sampling frame (e.g., omission of the homeless, many of whom are heavy drinkers), nonresponse within households, and underreporting by respondents.

Further doubt about these estimates is raised by other work done by the same research organization (Abt Associates, 1997) in Cook County. Using a more elaborate set of filters for observing frequent users of cocaine and heroin, the researchers produced prevalence estimates for weekly consumption in the county that were almost three times higher than those previously estimated. Since prevalence of heavy use is an important driver of both quantity and expenditure estimates, these findings, if replicated in other areas, could substantially raise the totals.

None of this is to fault the ONDCP-sponsored work. It does, however, point to the frailty of the enterprise of measuring illegal drug market activity. The systematic and random errors are large enough and so little understood that even the direction of year-to-year variations is in question. For example, the ONDCP estimates show a decline in heroin consumption between 1990 and 1991 of 17 percent (from 11.8 to 9.8 tons), yet prices were almost unchanged ($1,476 in 1990 and $1,470 in 1991), and other indicators of heroin use (e.g., emergency department mentions involving heroin) showed no decline. With a stable population of heroin addicts, it is difficult to account for large one-year interruptions to consumption that are unrelated to price.

Estimates of supply, using information about the areas under crop cultivation, production efficiency, and trafficking losses, have even less authority. For example, the ONDCP/Abt supply series for cocaine shows little change from 1988 to 1992; a sudden one-time drop, from 1993 to 1995, further reduces confidence, since no event occurred in 1992-1993 that might explain this. Moreover, there is a 1990-1991 decline in estimates of consumption (presumably related to the crackdown on the Medellin cartel in Colombia) that is not shown in the supply-side series. The series closest to the consumption estimates, "cocaine available for consumption in the United States," is consistently about one-third higher than estimated consumption.

In this instance it is not the lack of access to agency materials that seems to be the problem. The ONDCP estimates were developed with the full cooperation of U.S. federal agencies, which are thought to be the most well informed even for many producer countries. The U.S. estimates are cited in other national and international documents as the most authoritative sources. This points to the inherent difficulties of quantifying illegal market size, particularly from the supply side.

The United Nations Drug Control Program (UNDCP) has used these estimates and other data sources to generate an estimate of $400-500 billion for the global trade in illicit drugs (United Nations Drug Control Program, 1997). These figures, represented as international trade flows and comparable to trade in oil or automobiles, are hard to reconcile with estimates of the total number of drug users, most of whom are in poor countries, such as Iran, Pakistan, and Thailand (see Reuter, 1998). It is difficult to justify a global total of more than $150 billion, given the U.S. figures. Furthermore, this is clearly a measure of total expenditure; the trade element is probably less than 20 percent of that figure, producing a figure no more than one-tenth that cited by UNDCP.

The emphasis in these estimates (both U.S. and international) has been on revenues and, to a lesser extent, quantity. No attention has been given to estimating the number of sellers, certainly another important element of the harms arising from the transnational drug trade. There has been attention, however, to the estimation of another very basic factor in drug markets, namely the price elasticity of demand for cocaine, heroin, and marijuana—that is, the extent to which the demand varies with price (Saffer and Chaloupka, 1995; Grossman et al., in press). The finding has been that these elasticities are substantially higher than one might expect for dependency-creating substances and quite comparable to those for other legitimate goods. These estimates have used large population surveys, such as Monitoring the Future and the National Household Survey on Drug Abuse. Note, however, that these elasticities are with respect to prevalence of use of the drug, not quantity consumed. True price elasticities remain to be estimated.

No effort has been made to estimate an equally important elasticity, namely the price elasticity of supply. Assumptions that it is generally very high have been embedded in simulation models (e.g., Kennedy et al., 1992) with general theoretical and anecdotal support, but they have not been validated empirically.

The DEA collects data on prices at different points in the distribution chain; for example, in the cocaine trade from high-level wholesale (10 kilograms) to a retail sale (100 milligrams). These price data provide an important insight into the markets because they enable one to infer the allocation of revenues across levels of distribution; if the price for an ounce of pure cocaine is $700 ($25 per gram) and the street price is $80 for an 80 percent pure gram ($100 per gram), then the revenues to the low-level wholesaler and retailer account for 75 percent of the total (Caulkins and Reuter, 1998). This may have great policy significance, although there are major analytic issues to be settled about the relationship between high-level enforcement and retail prices (Caulkins, 1990). For those interested in transnational flows, it would be particularly useful to have figures on import prices, generally involving sales in the United States at the 100 kilogram level for cocaine and 10 kilogram level for heroin; the available data are sparse because such transactions are few and particularly difficult to monitor.

In summary, we have a rough estimate of expenditures on illicit drugs (a few tens of billions of dollars), total consumption of specific drugs (e.g., the mid-hundreds of tons of cocaine), and decent estimates of who receives these revenues at different levels of the distribution system. Scale is best estimated from studies of consumption, whereas allocation comes from data on the supply side.

OTHER MARKETS

For most transnational organized crime activities, there are simply no systematic estimates of size. For example, although the Immigration and Naturalization Service has recently made attempts to estimate the number of illegal immigrants inside the United States (Immigration and Naturalization Service, 1997), it has not attempted to estimate either the number entering as the result of organized smuggling activities or the revenues generated by such smuggling.[3] The International Criminal Police Organization (INTERPOL) estimates trafficking in animals at $5 billion globally, with $1.2 billion of that accounted for by U.S. purchases (*Inter Press Service*, July 21, 1995, cited in Williams, 1998); however, the estimate has no systematic, documented base.

Even money laundering, generally thought to be the single most important activity in terms of international money flows, has defied revenue estimates. The principal international organization dealing with these matters, the Financial Action Task Force (1996) of the Organization for Economic Co-operation and Development, reported that "the vast majority of members lack sufficient data to support credible estimates" (p. 2). At best those countries could report seizures from narcotics transactions or money laundering transactions. One (unnamed) nation offered an estimate, but only a very vague description was provided of the method used to generate it.

Feige and others have used discrepancies in aggregate economic statis-

---

[3]Chin (1998:25) reports, without citation, a senior immigration official's statement that Chinese organized crime groups make $3 billion from human smuggling operations.

tics to measure the extent of unrecorded economic activity, some of which is criminal (e.g., Feige, 1996). It has not proven possible to use these methods to separate out the informal but legal from the wholly illegal activities or determine how much involves cross-border flows. Similarly, the ubiquitous payment of bribes to foreign officials by multinational corporations, although subject to investigation in numerous countries, has never been estimated.[4]

CONCLUSION

Transnational organized crime may be susceptible to measurement, but very little is currently available to suggest how the measurement task should be approached. One conclusion that might be weakly inferred from the attempts to estimate the scale of drug importing is that consumption-based estimates are likely to be stronger than supply-based estimates. However, the large population surveys that exist for drug use do not exist for other illicit commodities and services. Moreover, measuring other markets that have little in common (i.e., the smuggling of illegal immigrants, endangered species, or weapons) with any specificity may prove challenging because of low base rates of consumption compared with rates for drugs, for example. It seems clear that the measurement task will require very different data collection and analytic methods than have so far been available. These data problems are more fully discussed in Chapter 5.

---

[4]This statement is based on a review of Internet sites for the following organizations: Transparency International (http://www.transparency.org), and the Organization for Economic Cooperation and Development (OECD) (http://www.oecd.org).

4

Enforcement

The potential for grave harm to national security from transnational organized crime fuels great concern at the political level. Federal Bureau of Investigation (FBI) Director Louis Freeh and former Central Intelligence Agency (CIA) Director R. James Woolsey both have asserted that transnational organized crime threatens the national security interests of the United States and other nations, and places "the very fabric of democratic society" at risk everywhere (Raine and Cilluffo, 1994). From this perspective, law enforcement and national security become increasingly entangled. Transnational groups are seen as a new breed of criminal organization whose high-tech methodologies outstrip anything that law enforcement agencies have to stop them (Raine and Cilluffo, 1994). The spectre of access by terrorist groups (through transnational crime networks) to weapons of mass destruction further intensifies these fears. And the problems of definition, complexity, and measurement we have discussed lead many law enforcement and policy officials to see transnational crime as an intractable issue.

Workshop participants agreed, however, that putting the problem of transnational organized crime in perspective means that most of these activities are something less than a major threat to national security and fragile democracies around the globe. The alarmist view tends to obscure the important reality that there are separable elements in many of these offenses, that some are more serious and complex than others, and that many are detectable, although their investigation may be difficult.

A principal barrier to investigating these crimes is that governments have sovereign or exclusive power within their own borders and virtually none elsewhere (Nadelmann, 1993). Countries affected by these crimes differ in their political, social, economic, and legal systems and cultures. These differences generate friction for the police. Their law enforcement powers are severely restricted when a criminal investigation crosses the border, and their investigative efforts are complicated by a lack of understanding of political and legal structures and language.

Frequently there is confusion about who has jurisdiction over individual cases. This surfaces constantly in the illegal drug trade. Cases of drug selling, easily detectable by local police, almost certainly are connected to individual cooffenders or criminal networks in other U.S. jurisdictions and other countries. In some instances, local police investigate local dealers or suppliers, only to find that one or more federal agencies, including the military, or police from other countries, or INTERPOL are involved in the investigation at some level. When no agreements governing cooperation are in place, these situations create many opportunities for domestic and international organizational conflict among law enforcement agencies, jurisdictions, and countries (Schlegel, 1998). One workshop participant related an incident in which the FBI had an undercover operation in Miami directed against what turned out to be an undercover operation by the Drug Enforcement Agency. He was able to get information to both organizations that "it would be all badges." These situations are reported to occur with some regularity.

NEED FOR COOPERATIVE RELATIONSHIPS

The development of transnational police cooperation is an increasingly common response strategy to transnational organized crime. Cooperation is framed through high-level bilateral and multilateral assistance treaties with other nations. States may agree to exchange subject-matter experts and investigative expertise and to provide training for police. Treaties set out rules for the sharing of intelligence and other evidence and for determining jurisdiction in specific cases. They establish standards for investigative methods, the extradition of offenders, and the imposition of sanctions. Frequently, they involve the stationing of law enforcement personnel in embassies abroad or even the opening of a law enforcement headquarters or training facility in a foreign capital.

In response to the spread of transnational organized crime, the 1990s saw an unprecedented presence of U.S. law enforcement personnel in other countries. For example, over 100 U.S. law enforcement agents were stationed in U.S. embassies and consulates in Europe, and dozens of others were traveling there on temporary business (Nadelmann, 1993). This has resulted in a strong American influence on law enforcement practices in much of Western Europe, especially in pursuit of U.S. global drug control objectives. U.S. Department of Justice and U.S. military officials also have been active in drug interdiction efforts in South America and Mexico since the Bush administration in the late 1980s. These partnerships can work relatively well when the cooperating countries have well established law enforcement systems. In the context of police system modernization in emerging democracies, however, many problems of implementation can arise. These can be traced to the differences between Western expectations and the aspirations of emerging democracies, for example, those in Russia and Eastern Europe (Gregory, 1995), as well as other poor countries characterized by weak political systems and markets and official corruption.

ITALIAN-AMERICAN WORKING GROUP

The Italian-American Working Group formed in 1984 to target organized crime provides an example of a positive relationship between two countries with mature legal and investigative systems. During the 1970s the center of heroin trafficking moved from France and its island of Corsica to Sicily, where it operated under the then virtually impenetrable Sicilian La Cosa Nostra. The power structure of the Sicilian Mafia was being fundamentally altered at that time to support the huge international trade in illegal narcotics. Numerous previous narcotics investigations had involved both Italy and the United States, but prosecutions were usually brought in only one country, and the vast differences in the two countries' legal systems led to competition rather than cooperation (Martin, 1998).[1]

In the 1980s organized crime groups in Italy became stronger through a series of activities, including the murder of high officials (including the chief prosecutor of Palermo); violent infighting among Mafia factions, resulting in many deaths; and the development of political coalitions designed to keep the Communists out of power. Against this backdrop, the

---

[1] Most of the information in this section is taken from the case study by Martin (1998).

United States and Italy decided to develop a cooperative relationship that would be able to challenge organized crime and its control of drug trafficking (Martin, 1998). New treaties were developed to speed up the extradition process; to make possible the rapid exchange of investigative information and the execution of searches and seizures; and the direct, confidential exchange of virtually every type of law enforcement information.

Overcoming the barriers to this level of cooperation required approval at the highest levels in both governments. The working group was formed to take advantage of the cooperative relationships that had been formed at the working level. Its meetings, held semiannually from 1984 to 1990, frequently included the top law enforcement official of both countries, the U.S. attorney general, and the Italian minister of interior. The directors of major law enforcement agencies from both countries also attended. The group provided a framework of support for the law enforcement agencies and paved the way for improved prosecutions, for example, by moving vulnerable witnesses to the United States where, under U.S. law, they could be protected and offered immunity from prosecution.

The functioning of the Italian-American Working Group was illustrated by a case dubbed "the pizza connection," a massive drug trafficking operation from Sicily to New York, uncovered by investigators and prosecutors. In Richard Martin's words, "What started as a limited exchange of information about particular individuals became an open flow of communication that functioned almost as if there were no frontiers or legal barriers between the countries" (Martin 1998:8). In another example, the Buscetta case, which involved the first Sicilian Mafia member ever to testify in public, the United States guaranteed his protection, when Italy, under its own laws, was unable to do so. Martin observed that the most important lesson learned by the working group was the need for agents at the managerial level to spend time together, to learn from each other, and to overcome suspicions about information sharing.

By the 1990s, the working group meetings became less frequent, but the U.S. law enforcement presence in Italy was by then well established. Some 30 federal law enforcement representatives were stationed in the U.S. embassy in Rome. These included agents from the Drug Enforcement Administration, the Federal Bureau of Investigation, the Secret Service, the Customs Service, Internal Revenue Service, the Immigration and Naturalization Service, multiple military investigative agencies, and a former federal prosecutor representing the attorney general (Nadelmann, 1993). The Italian-American Working Group has been revived recently to address new problems common to each country, particularly Russian organized crime and new Mafia support of emerging crime groups (Martin, 1998).

RUSSIA

Cross-national cooperation becomes a greater challenge when a state lacks a strong criminal justice system based on the rule of law. In Russia, for example, the weakness of the state after the fall of communism has provided opportunities for organized crime and corruption. The unprecedented process of privatizing previously nationalized property, businesses, and institutions created an advantage for Russian criminals, who had amassed certain resources and capabilities originating from black market operations during the days of the Communist regime. Much of the private wealth and property in Russia is now thought to be in the hands of these organized criminal groups.

Although much has been made of the new Russian state's weakness in contract enforcement and the growing role of organized criminal groups in taking on that function, comparably important is the lack of a statutory base to prevent criminal activities from taking place. In Russia, there are no criminal penalties for phony businesses, fictitious bankruptcies, or other socially dangerous practices in a market economy. No legislation against organized crime has been passed. Law enforcement cannot target criminal organizations or use measures such as witness protection and informants to enhance their capacity for a more effective response to organized crime. There is little financial or social support for law enforcement itself (Williams, 1996).

Difficulties in the cooperative relationship between Russia and the United States were manifested by an attempt at joint efforts to prevent smuggling of nuclear materials under Russian control. This issue came to U.S. attention as a result of high-profile cases in Germany, where documented cases were reported to be on the rise (Gregory, 1995). In addition to its law enforcement problems, other Russian internal factors contributed to a dangerously weak intergovernmental response. A 1994 report from the Russian Federation Atomic Energy Regulatory Authority found that no state system of control and accounting of nuclear material existed in Russia. Moreover, during a period when Russian political and administrative systems were undergoing major transformation, responsibility for the protection of nuclear materials and installations was divided among four separate government bureaucracies, and coordination was at a minimum. These structural weaknesses were made worse by cultural and political issues—a perceived need to maintain national pride, the sensitivities of the military, and a general mistrust of Western motives.

Subsequently, on the U.S. side, plans to help the Russian Federation improve its nuclear security stalled. As with the Russian Federation, the three major departments of government responsible for fostering U.S.-Russian collaboration "pursued separate and sometimes poorly coordinated efforts to initiate cooperation with the Russian bureaucracies involved" (Gregory, 1995:127). Thus, in contrast to the situation in Italy, there was no central U.S. mechanism to share intelligence or investigative expertise on these crimes. A plan to open an FBI office in Moscow degraded into a limited agreement that two FBI agents could work from the U.S. embassy there (Gregory, 1995). The construction in Russia of a large nuclear arsenal and the existence of powerful organized crime groups make enforcement efforts there uniquely important to the United States. Finding means for more effectively transferring U.S. enforcement expertise to help the Russian state reduce the power of organized crime is a matter of some urgency.

BARRIERS TO COOPERATION

An underdeveloped issue is whether an organization like the Italian-American Working Group is unique to the circumstances that gave rise to it and the relationships that grew out of those circumstances, or whether it can serve as a model for other successful partnerships. Workshop participants noted that the political will must exist among senior officials in a country to target transnational organized crime and to develop the cooperative relationships required for successful investigations and prosecutions. The success of the Italian-American Working Group partly depended on the sophisticated law enforcement information systems, legal systems, and education systems of the two countries. Many poor countries and emerging democracies lack this basic infrastructure. Other potential barriers are the presence of endemic corruption; the level of nationalism; whether treaties governing law enforcement processes can be negotiated; and whether domestic policy objectives conflict with the development of common law enforcement goals (Martin, 1998).

Workshop participants discussed American-style law enforcement as a barrier to cooperation, noting that some countries object to American methods of undercover work that has the potential for entrapment (e.g., the use of informants, buy-and-bust operations). Others noted that the United States increasingly is asked to provide investigative training and technical assistance in both Western and Eastern European countries in response to rising transnational and domestic crime rates there. Despite concerns about entrapment and invasion of privacy, many of these methods have been adopted in Europe because they produce results. Using these methods makes cases, effects seizures, puts people in jail, and results in at least a perceived reduction in harm. Concern also was expressed about the friction and organizational rivalries consequent to the pervasive U.S. law enforcement presence overseas—a presence that supports the extensive targeting of organized crime, intelligence collection efforts, new police training efforts, and prosecutions led by the U.S. Department of Justice. One participant lamented the underrepresentation of Customs officials at the workshop. As a major point of potential contact between transnational crimes and official law enforcement, investigations often begin with Customs. Participants noted that organizational rivalry and friction frequently arise between police investigators and Customs officials at international borders, citing examples on the German-French border and the U.S.-Mexican and U.S.-Canadian borders.

DOMINANCE OF FEDERAL AGENCIES

In the United States, the responsibility for responding to transnational crime has increasingly fallen to the federal government and, as noted above, it involves diplomats and intelligence agents as well as law enforcement. There are several reasons for this. Foremost, the cultural, political, legal, and language differences among different nations can be handled only at the federal level. State and local governments lack the authority to enter into treaties and the requisite knowledge of international law to deal with these issues on their own. They must relinquish jurisdiction to the federal government in matters of national security. And the resources, expertise, and personnel required to investigate and prosecute organizationally and technologically complex cases reside—with only a few exceptions—at the federal rather than the state and local levels.

Federal intelligence agencies also are heavily involved in investigating extraterritorial violations of U.S. laws—particularly export control violations and weapons smuggling—that intermingle criminal justice and national security interests. However, a state's pursuit of a particular international law enforcement agenda is often constrained by the fact that criminal justice objectives are rarely predominant on its foreign policy agenda. Even among closely allied states, conflicting political interests and viewpoints, often involving powerful domestic constituencies, may impede cooperation in law enforcement matters (Nadelmann, 1993). Congressional committees have routinely complained about the lack of attention to drug control issues by U.S. ambassadors in major drug-producing or transshipment countries, such as Pakistan, Turkey, and even, until recently, Mexico. The Mexican outrage about a major money-laundering investigation by U.S. agencies of Mexican banks, in which the Mexican authorities were not even informed, has left a lingering bitterness at the highest levels of the Mexican government.

PROBLEMS FOR LOCAL LAW ENFORCEMENT

Participants noted that attempting to deal with transnational crime at the local level highlights the weaknesses of traditional police work. Local law enforcement generally is organized to respond to complaints of individual citizens or small groups in the community that have been harmed by crime directly. These are usually straightforward criminal acts, well described in the criminal codes of most states and municipalities. They involve single offenders, small offender groups, or local youth gangs. They are relatively simple to investigate and do not require the level of professional education or highly specialized investigative training needed for sophisticated offenses—computer crime or securities fraud, for example. Successful prosecution depends on the presence of the elements of a crime—that the criminal harm can be demonstrated and the criminal intent of the offender established beyond a reasonable doubt. Professional expertise, if required at all, is usually introduced in the prosecution phase through the testimony of expert witnesses, rather than in the investigation phase.

Some transnational crimes appear to fit this model of street crime—street sales of drugs, some smuggling cases, some homicides. Frequently, local police are unaware of transnational factors associated with these offenses or treat them as unimportant. They see a street vendor selling stolen designer clothing or designer knockoffs, but do not connect that act with transnational smuggling or forced labor. Their interest and training lie in protecting the legitimate manufacturer or owner of the stolen goods, not in tracking down smugglers, or tracing evidence or laundered money back to organized crime bosses in foreign countries.

The transnational nature of these offenses adds organizational, technological, and spatial complexity to the investigative task. These crimes often involve systematic and complicated forms of economic criminality that require arcane knowledge. Smugglers hide their illegal profits by engaging in a legal activity, such as wiring money to offshore accounts or investing in legitimate businesses. Many frauds exploit opportunities created by legitimate economic behavior by mimicking acceptable legal behavior, such as the filing of health insurance claims. Harm from these crimes is often diffuse and victims hard to identify. Using legal means to accomplish criminal goals can obscure the element of criminal intent, which is necessary for the prosecution of a case.

Given these difficulties, workshop participants debated whether a state or local role was even appropriate for these kinds of crimes. Most participants agreed that transnational crimes of serious interest involve sophisticated white-collar and organized offenses of significant scope, and that, in all probability, these crimes are on the rise. Several participants noted that the local law enforcement interface with these crimes occurs on the demand side, where the market has its most visible manifestation, and that it is important to think of ways to change traditional policing to respond to these opportunities for detection and control. Others, however, felt that local law enforcement agencies are, for the most part, too small and too focused on basic community safety to ever have the capacity to respond effectively to these crimes. In addition, the involvement of state and local authorities could result in unacceptable levels of diffusion of sensitive information about cases. This could create both corruption and security problems at the local level, with the potential to affect federal and international investigative efforts.

Part of the problem for all levels of law enforcement, in responding to these offenses, lies in whether illegal markets can be significantly diminished and, if so, how. Some markets are eliminated, or at least significantly decreased, without effective law enforcement. Rather the declines stem from social and economic changes: altered public attitudes, scientific advances, or shifts in profitability.

For example, there have been major changes in the prevalence of marijuana use in the U.S. population over the past 25 years, which seem unrelated to law enforcement. The long decline in marijuana use during the 1980s did not represent the consequences of tougher enforcement; indeed, marijuana arrest rates substantially declined. The sharp upturn in adolescent use rates from 1993 to 1997 occurred at the same time that marijuana possession arrest rates also rose dramatically. Fashions, not susceptible to government influence, seem to be as important as any other set of factors.

This difficulty in controlling illegal markets can affect policy. In another example, recent changes in the attitudes of African governments toward protecting elephants from poachers were driven not by law enforcement, but by the increasing economic value of nonconsumptive uses of elephants, especially with regard to tourism (Nadelmann, 1990). These economic forces, plus public, moral condemnation of elephant killing, led to a global ban, backed by the U.S. government and conservationist groups, on the sale and purchase of new ivory and the subsequent creation of illegal ivory markets. Some conservationists, as well as park managers and governments in southern Africa where elephant populations have stabilized or even grown, oppose the ban. They have insisted that southern Africans should not have to forgo ivory revenues that are channeled back to the national parks because other Africans have mismanaged their ivory resources. Efforts have been under way for several years to create a substitute ivory composed of ceramics, but many consumers, especially the Japanese, who buy more than 40 percent of Africa's ivory, may continue to insist on the real thing (Nadelmann, 1990).

Although the influence of social and economic forces in diminishing illegal markets may be readily apparent, the impact of law enforcement activities is not. Almost no research information exists on the results of law enforcement efforts to disrupt and decrease these illegal markets. Law enforcement takes credit for recent declines in cocaine use in the United States, but in fact no research exists on the causes, which remain unknown. Workshop participants noted that recent work on problem-solving policing and the disruption of drug markets shows some promise, although the disruption is to physical marketplaces for the most part rather than the markets themselves. In the end, local, federal, and international agencies may be effective in disrupting transnational markets only if they act cooperatively, rather than singly or in competition with one another, and only if they are able to devise creative prevention and deterrence strategies to complement traditional enforcement activities. For complex organized and white-collar offenses, these strategies may involve civil and regulatory actions in lieu of or concurrent with criminal prosecutions, for example.

CURRENT AD HOC ARRANGEMENTS

One response to the inadequacies of local law enforcement agencies with regard to transnational offenses is the formation of multiagency task forces. These task forces typically involve formalized relationships between agencies with specific agreements that pertain to a specific case or type of crime. Task forces can provide a structure for pooling resources and information and for the development of guidelines for interagency cooperation in complex cases.

Many law enforcement agencies view task forces with skepticism, however. Task forces can create a drain on already-limited time and resources, and their continued success depends on a steady flow of important and solvable cases or investigative breakthroughs on a big case that focus attention and provide a set of common problems to work on. Schlegel (1998) notes that task forces are typically, formed to demonstrate that attention is being given to a problem, with no real effort to define the tasks of the group, the functions of the participating agencies, or even the general organizational mission (Schlegel, 1998).

Although some task forces achieve their goals in solving cases, many others appear simply to meet periodically, with little actual coordination or cooperation in solving cases taking place. One participant noted that some agencies appear to see task forces as vehicles to get more resources. Workshop participants urged caution in using "tip of the iceberg" metaphors and other exaggerated language to describe transnational crime problems. There was concern that one or two cases involving immigrant offenders can be used to "create a problem" at the local level, which in turn results in the creation of an expensive and unnecessary investigative unit or multiagency task force.

CONCLUSION

The workshop discussion yielded important insights about law enforcement efforts and their implications for future research. The federal government is exploring a variety of methods for increasing its capability to control transnational crime; the focus of that effort is investigation rather than long-term reduction. Such investigations require substantial cooperation between the countries touched by individual crimes, and it seems important that cooperation be clearly spelled out in formal agreements. Research efforts tied to this investigative focus may prove useful in developing better information about transnational crimes and justice system responses to them.

At the local level in the United States, there is little awareness of transnational crime, although it appears that local participation would benefit investigations, since transnational offenses frequently first surface there. Thus, successful identification, investigation, and prosecution of transnational crimes may require cooperation not only between countries, but also (in the United States) between federal and local levels of government. However, given the limited capacities and authority of local law enforcement agencies to fully investigate these matters, their role must be carefully thought out. The clear articulation of goals, responsibilities, and the tasks appropriate to each jurisdictional level, along with careful documentation of joint investigative efforts, could serve as a basis for a program of evaluation research in this area.

5

Research Agenda

Transnational crime is clearly a social and legal problem worthy of attention; there are too many documented instances and too much credible theory to dismiss it as mere journalistic sensationalism. However, it is less clear as to just how large it is, whether it is expanding rapidly, poses important new threats to American society, or requires major changes in U.S. law enforcement. Nor is there much understanding of what conditions foster it. A research agenda must address all of these matters: how it should be described and measured, how it affects American society, and what are the means of controlling it.

The underlying question is what can the United States do to keep transnational organized crime to a low level. A research agenda with this theme would have at least three elements: problem identification, development of data sources and possible methodologies for empirical and theoretical analysis, and assessment of the consequences of regulation and control. Separating the elements is, of course, not so neat. For example, the identification of the problem to be studied has implications for the appropriate choice of datasets and methodologies, and what can be studied is very much a function of the datasets that are likely to be available. The following agenda draws on discussions characterized by divergent views; hence it allows for alternative emphases among and within the various topics.

PROBLEM IDENTIFICATION

Scope

The focus of the workshop was on transnational organized crime, primarily as it affects the United States, either domestically or in terms of U.S. foreign interests. In Mexico and Russia, internal organized crime is important since it raises issues of specific concern to the United States.

It is increasingly evident that Mexico has a major organized crime problem. Not only are large sums being earned by drug-trafficking organizations, but also those organizations are corrupting very high levels of the government and may be responsible for a number of important political assassinations.[1] Some U.S. officials are more willing to collaborate even with Colombian enforcement agencies than with those of Mexico, because the corruption of the latter has been so pervasive. Given that the United States and Mexico are so intertwined economically, politically, and culturally, a Mexican organized crime problem becomes a major U.S. concern. For example, the United States, even in the face of the requirements for open borders of the North American Free Trade Agreement (NAFTA), has continued to inspect Mexican truck trafficking because of concerns about the lack of integrity in Mexican border controls).

The concern with Russia has related origins. It is not as former adversary but as the owner of a substantial nuclear stockpile under weak security conditions that the United States has a special interest in how organized crime weakens the governance of Russia. Russia's biological weapons program is also a concern. The U.S. government has a variety of programs aimed at strengthening the institutions of government and civil society in Russia in order to prevent either the rise of a hostile government or the leakage of the nuclear (or biological weapons) capability (materials or skilled personnel) to other adversaries, such as Iran, Iraq, and Libya, or to terrorist groups. Thus an American research program on transnational organized crime should include coverage of organized crime in Mexico and Russia.

A second issue of scope needs to be addressed. Many important issues involved in transnational organized crime are more appropriately the subject of investigation rather than research, usually because they involve clas-

---

[1] A useful source on these matters are the Mexico chapters of the U.S. Department of State's *International Narcotics Control Strategy Report*.

sified materials or require the peculiar legal capabilities of law enforcement agencies. For example, U.S. intelligence organizations have in the past collaborated with drug-smuggling organizations, in both Asia and Latin America. Social scientists may contribute to understanding these phenomena and what mechanisms generate them or could lead to earlier detection, but the basic task of developing knowledge is likely to be the province of Congress or agencies such as the inspector general of the Central Intelligence Agency.

Harms of Transnational Organized Crime

A research agenda aimed at policy making should include research on the nature of the adverse consequences of various forms of transnational organized crimes, which would help guide resource allocation decisions, both between transnational organized crime and other crimes and within transnational organized crime. Here we identify the harms that prior research suggests deserve more attention.

National Security

As reflected in Presidential Decision Directive 42, already mentioned, transnational organized crime is asserted to be a national security threat. For example, Jonathan Winer, a senior State Department official, testified that "transnational organized crime threatens America's national security and foreign policy interests in a number of regions of the world, undermining legitimate economies and threatening emerging democracies."[2] This is offered as a justification for the leadership role that the State Department has taken in various overseas programmatic activities in this functional area, such as the International Law Enforcement Training Academy in Budapest.

An appropriate research task is assessing what forms of transnational organized crime threaten national security and in what ways. For example, it is asserted that money laundering threatens global liquidity and the soundness of the global financial system. Although in theory money laundering on a large-enough scale could indeed pose such a threat, it is worth examining whether in any instance it has had a major impact and the circumstances under which that might yet occur.

---

[2]Winer Testimony before the Senate Caucus on International Narcotics Control of the Subcommittee on Trade of the Senate Finance Committee, July 30, 1996.

Clearly drug trafficking has had a substantial impact on some producer nations' security. The government of Burma over a 30-year period has been engaged in a struggle with irredentist (rebel) groups that are financed substantially by the drug trade; the Sendero Luminoso movement in Peru was better able to fight the government in the 1980s because of its taxation of the local coca industry. Colombia, with many sources of large-scale violence, has had its internal security efforts further compromised by drug traffickers. But apart from Mexico and Russia, it is much more difficult to see how these phenomena imperil U.S. national security, except under the very broadest of definitions, and that U.S. research is needed.

International Treaties

The rising concern about global environmental protection has created new international regulations and treaties that are dependent on compliance by many nations. The Montreal Protocol on chlorofluorocarbons (CFCs) is an early example of a successful treaty of this type. Any regulation offers the opportunity for profitable evasion, but, since treaties often impose lighter restrictions on poorer nations, niches are created for transnational organized crime activities that undermine the agreement. The Convention on International Trade in Endangered Species of Wild Flora and Fauna (CITE) is another agreement, intended to control a trade that usually involves purchasers in rich countries buying from suppliers in very poor nations. Understanding the impact of transnational organized crime on the effectiveness of these agreements may be an important topic.

In a perverse way, transnational organized crime also sometimes represents a threat when barriers are being lowered. NAFTA was designed to facilitate trade between the United States, Canada, and Mexico and the elimination of numerous barriers. That should have reduced the role of criminal organizations. However, NAFTA's continuation is dependent on popular support, which may be withdrawn in the United States to the extent that drug traffickers and smugglers of immigrants seem able to benefit from the easier rules for crossing the U.S.-Mexican border.

Increasing U.S. Criminal Victimization

As a rich nation, the United States is an attractive target for crime. For example, cars stolen for sale in poorer countries, by expanding the demand for car theft, worsen the crime problem in the United States. Such theft presents lower risk for the thieves than does sale to domestic purchasers of stolen cars, because recovery from the ultimate buyer is so much less likely once the car has left the country. Insurance spreads that cost but also raises it by insurers' administrative and managerial expenses.

Intellectual property theft constitutes perhaps the most significant of these transnational losses for the United States. Industry estimates, which partake of advocacy but surely have some foundation, are that the international piracy of software and recordings results in the loss of billions of dollars for U.S. corporations (Dertouzos et al., 1999). Here the interaction of criminal and legitimate organizations is particularly troubling. The marketing of these pirated products in the United States or elsewhere is done primarily by legal business corporations. How many and what kinds of firms are involved in these activities and how much is known by the owners or senior executives are reasonable questions.

Worsening America's Drug Problem

No doubt the removal of foreign supplies from the U.S. market for illicit drugs would result in some substitution of domestically produced synthetics. However, analysis of changes in drug abuse indicators following three incidents of disruption of foreign drug supplies suggests that the substitution is far from complete; for example, more opiate users sought treatment after the mid-1970s reduction in heroin imports, even though pharmacological substitutes were available from domestic sources (Reuter, 1992). Thus the extent to which transnational organized crime increases crime and drug-related mortality and morbidity in the United States should receive some research attention.

Corruption

Transnational organized crime may have a substantial impact on government corruption, particularly at the federal level. Cross-border smuggling of many kinds exposes border agents, including military personnel, to considerable temptation. Transnational organized crime may facilitate corruption by lowering transaction costs; a single negotiation can establish the schedule of payments for a series of shipments, rather than expose the agent to the risks of repeated contact and negotiations with individual smugglers. It is also possible that transnational organized crime can purchase protection more efficiently at the local level for the same reason, but its comparative advantage in that respect looks less distinctive. The nature and scope of government corruption related to transnational crime is an appropriate subject for future research.

Loss of Border Control

A nation is partly defined by its ability to control who and what crosses its borders. Smuggling is inevitable for a large, wealthy country with increasingly strong trading relations with the rest of the world. Powerful transnational organized crime may substantially exacerbate both illegal border crossings (whether for the purpose of immigration or for more opportunistic criminal activities) and smuggling of goods either prohibited (e.g., protected species) or subject to other restrictions (textiles from a nation whose legal imports already meet quota levels). Better estimates of illicit goods and illegal immigrants smuggled across U.S. borders is an important element of a research agenda on transnational crime.

Beneficiaries

Transnational organized crime, precisely because it so often involves the servicing of markets, is not simply an involuntary transfer of assets. It also is income-generating. Thus some foreign governments are ambivalent, because some forms of transnational organized crime create employment and bring in dollars. For example, in Bolivia a substantial fraction of its peasant population has weak economic alternatives, particularly in areas, such as the Chapare, that have developed specifically for coca growing (Clawson and Lee, 1996). The Bolivian government has manifested a reluctance to take strong actions to reduce this production. Similarly, some Asian nations, including China, have clearly been ambivalent about the suppression of software piracy, as demonstrated in U.S.-China trade negotiations in recent years. In that case, it is not only producers who benefit but also customers in those countries in which software is so much more cheaply available.

This list, though incomplete, suggests that the consequences of transnational organized crime are potentially many and varied. Describing and classifying them are preliminary steps to measurement and should form an important part of research activities.

DATA SOURCES

Official Records

Official records such as court and regulatory proceedings must be an important source of information. They are frequently highly detailed and, at least in the United States, accessible public information. The trials of the major U.S. Mafia figures in the 1980s generated a vast number of public records, although apparently they have been little used for research.[3] In Italy, similar records, augmented by interviews with the principal informants (*pentitti*), have already generated a number of studies that provide considerable insight into the workings, both national and international, of Italian organized crime (e.g., Gambetta, 1993; Paoli, 1997).

Some caveats are in order when using such data, however. Court records report on a small and unrepresentative set of activities, usually the most serious ones. Even in the population of actual prosecutions, itself unrepresentative of all criminal activities of these enterprises, most cases do not go to trial but are settled through plea bargains, which generate little public information beyond the indictment itself. Most indictments identify a set of specific criminal acts that provide only modest illumination of the underlying organization, although some prosecutors do use the indictment document to reveal much of the relevant evidence.

Nevertheless, official, agency-generated records are currently one of the best sources of useful data on transnational crime.

Investigative Records

Some scholars have been able to obtain investigative records from agencies for purposes of researching organized crime (e.g., Cressey, 1969; Haller, 1991). Such access is highly opportunistic, dependent on the whims of the agency and on the personal skills and connections of the researcher, even with industrious use of the Freedom of Information Act. These records may indeed constitute an important source of data, though these access problems may stymie their extensive use in a research program. Also, like court records, they present problems of agency bias. Investigation is not

---

[3]More from these transcripts can be found in the popular literature; see, for example, Blum and Todd (1995).

random (and should not be) but it is difficult to determine the consequences of the agency's choices as a sampling strategy, so to speak.

Ethnographic Studies and Surveys

Ko-Lin Chin has conducted a number of studies of Chinese organized crime in the United States, using interviews with community members as a principal data source (Chin, 1990, 1996). He has also conducted a mail survey of gang members and was able to obtain some information about their criminal activities by that means. Patricia and Peter Adler (Adler and Adler, 1985) described the organization of the cocaine trade in the late 1970s by observation of participants whom they had met socially.

Ethnographic studies and surveys are considered jointly because they derive information in the field. Both are valuable, but each has important limitations. On one hand, surveys are expensive and subject to particularly serious problems of nonresponse (exacerbated by the sensitivity of the subject) and gaps in the sampling frame (because many subjects are undocumented aliens). On the other hand, ethnographic work is labor-intensive and mostly suitable for the low end or street level of a trade (see, e.g., Curtis and Svirdoff, 1994), which may not yield much information about the transnational aspects. The multiplicity of languages used by the varied national groups involved in transnational organized crime also complicates this kind of research. However, when well done, ethnographic research provides detailed knowledge that cannot be captured in surveys or other empirical studies.

Informants

Related to ethnography is the use of informants, whether recruited through an agency (e.g., Haller, 1991) or by personal contacts (e.g., Ianni, 1972). The distinction is not a sharp one, but the informant may be interviewed in circumstances very distant from his or her natural setting, whereas ethnographers are generally rooted in the naturalistic setting of those providing the information. Informants may also be recruited in prisons, although again there is serious question of how representative they are of the larger participant population (see, e.g., Reuter and Haaga, 1989).

Financial Records of Illegal Enterprises

Some investigations result in the seizure of the financial records of illegal enterprises, particularly larger ones that use computers for such purposes. Only a little use has been made of these for the study of domestic drug distribution (e.g., Levitt and Venkatesh, 1998), but they can provide valuable descriptive information. One of their attractions is that investigative agencies are likely to regard financial records as less sensitive than records on individuals.

Other Sources

Transcripts from electronic surveillance can provide a great deal of information about operations. Sometimes even when they are not included in court transcripts, they can be obtained for research. Investigators, particularly those who have worked under cover for long periods, can prove at least as useful as criminal informants. They may have less understanding of the context of events, but they are likely to be more observant and capable of providing analytically coherent accounts. Individual prosecutors may also provide important data concerning cases (without specific names) that they did not pursue to court.

In summary, there are numerous potential data sources for the study of transnational organized crime. Each has substantial weaknesses, and most have an opportunistic element, since they are from operational sources. However, taken jointly and using methods to combine them, they may allow the development of a credible and multifaceted description of the activities of transnational organized crime.

TOPICS

Of course, to be useful for policy, the research would go beyond the descriptive and also attempt to answer more analytic and causal questions, particularly related to enforcement.

Conditions Promoting Transnational Organized Crime

What conditions facilitate the development of transnational organized crime? Passas (1998) has suggested that a principal factor is the existence of "criminogenic asymmetries," that is, differences among nations in laws or regulations or in the effectiveness of enforcement. Thus one nation may provide a safe haven, or at least a safer haven, for conducting criminal activities in the other. Certainly this applies to the international drug market. Coca could readily be grown in the United States (as it has been in Java, Bengal, and Taiwan at various times in the 20th century), but the much lower risk of sanction in the Andean nations, along with cheaper land labor, has allowed them to be the dominant production centers for the U.S. market. Similarly, weak efforts at vehicle identification and theft in Eastern Europe and Latin America facilitate the exporting of stolen cars from Western Europe and the United States. The hypothesis proposed by Passas offers a starting point for study of what facilitates and impedes the growth of transnational organized crime.

Immigration, both its numbers and characteristics, is also potentially an important factor, but much may depend on the strength and stability of government in the sending country, especially the firmness of the rule of law and the specificity of legislation targeting criminal activities. The opaqueness of many immigrant communities to policing allows organized crime networks to flourish in a relatively safe setting. The extent to which the receiving country is open to immigrants, providing opportunities for the learning of language, culture, and new skills and a niche in the legal economy, may influence the extent to which organized crime can gain a foothold in immigrant neighborhoods. It would be important to examine the roles of the sending country's economic and political conditions, the size and geographic distribution of immigrants in the United States, the speed of economic and linguistic assimilation into the broader community, and political traditions in the sender countries.

Prices

Prices are an important element of any illegal market. They affect who purchases the incentives for participation, and the damage that the activities cause in each nation. That Chinese immigrants apparently pay smugglers $45,000 per person for successful entry into the United States (Chin, 1998:25), compared with quite nominal amounts paid by Mexicans seeking illegal entry into the country (Cornelius, 1989) may generate more violence (both by smugglers in protection of their cargo and in collecting these large debts) and corruption.

Not only do price data need to be collected in a systematic fashion, perhaps with informant debriefings as a major source, but they also need systematic analysis. For example, how much is enforcement able to influence price? A simple framework has been developed (though not yet tested) for the relationship between drug prices and drug enforcement (Reuter and Kleiman, 1986). That may be generalizable to other illegal market activities, including money laundering. Prices are also essential for analysis of demand and supply factors that might lead to identification of other factors susceptible to regulatory control.

Enforcement

Description and Classification

A possible starting point is a listing and systematic classification of what constitutes enforcement activities relevant to the control of transnational organized crime. It will be primarily a list of federal efforts. Complementary to that list is a conceptual framework that suggests how particular programs and interventions might be expected to affect transnational organized crime—that is, by what means each may affect particular aspects of transnational organized crime. In terms of local enforcement, more research attention would be needed on the nature and frequency of transnational organized crime and white-collar crimes that come to police attention, as well as the conditions that give rise to them. Such epidemiological or surveillance measures might support theory development, provide for greater clarity with respect to the goals of enforcement and prevention responses, and lead to more precise outcome measures.

Outcome Measures

Inasmuch as a program specifically targets transnational organized crime, it will be necessary to develop measures to assess its success beyond the apprehension and sanctioning of the targeted individuals and organizations. These include the classic elements of deterrence, general and specific, as well as the opening (through churning) or closing (because of the incapacitation of a critical link) of new opportunities. Attention should also be paid to unintended consequences. Money-laundering controls may produce transaction costs that are borne by poor persons (as with limiting the amount of cash that can be collected at urban bodega) or that reduce the competitiveness of U.S. financial institutions.

Preventive Strategies

Recently there has developed a line of analysis and innovation focused on "opportunity blocking" for organized crime (Jacobs et al., 1994). It represents an understanding that much organized crime activity involving legitimate industries is the exploitation of opportunities that arise from the structure of contracting, regulation, or markets. Careful analysis of firms or industries to identify vulnerabilities may prevent the emergence of organized crime. This may have application to transnational organized crime and is an appropriate subject for research.

Prevention strategies that operate at a still broader level may be appropriate subjects for research, for example, more strategic policing of immigrant communities focused on preventing criminal groups from developing power over legitimate community institutions. This would need to be done in a way that recognizes the sensitivity of new immigrant communities to discriminatory enforcement, but research building on the frameworks developed in community policing may be helpful.

RESEARCH METHODS

No single research approach is likely to dominate in this area. At one level, as a workshop participant later suggested, the discussion could be characterized as a debate between "skeptic describers" and "quantifiers." At another level, it was about the choice of unit and the most appropriate social science discipline.

Economics must play a role because markets are such an important element of transnational criminal activities. But the standard economic approaches have their limits in settings in which violence and legal penalties serve as very discriminating selection mechanisms for participation. The visible hand of violence may make the invisible hand of competition less effective, although there are some major illegal markets in which that appears not to be the case (Reuter, 1983).

Economic approaches emphasize systematic modeling and measurement. Economists are reluctant to enter research fields without the kind of quantitative data that allow them to use the sophisticated techniques that are now the staple and requirements of publication in good journals. Data on transnational organized crime are not likely to reach that richness and density for some time. It is worth noting, however, the observation or injunction of Alfred Blumstein (Carnegie Mellon University) that "the way to get good data is to do something useful with bad data."

Other social sciences with more developed traditions for dealing with qualitative data have much to offer. Network analysis and other frames for the study of organization may generate a great deal of insight with the qualitative data that will be available for some time. Criminology provides a set of tools useful for the study of sanctioning effects. Williams (1998) has shown that international relations can offer important insights.

In a setting in which quantitative data are scarce but stories are numerous, case studies may prove a fruitful way to advance knowledge. Graham Alison's *Essence of Decision,* a study of decision making during the Cuban missile crisis, helped develop a new framework for analyzing government decision making (Alison, 1971). Its power derived in part from the richness of its description of the decision process. Case studies have a well-established role in many other fields of social science research, particularly related to crime (e.g., Klockars, 1975; Sutherland, 1937).

The Cuban missile crisis was atypical, perhaps the only time Armageddon was squarely faced by the U.S. government. That atypicality turned out to be analytically useful, because it threw so much of the process into stark relief. A detailed examination of a major transnational crime event or process may have the same power. For example, the Bank of Credit and Commerce International case, involving numerous nations, organizations, participants, and services around a fundamentally fraudulent institution, could serve this role. Various agencies have published detailed reports on the investigations they conducted on specific aspects of the case, both in the United States and elsewhere, and Passas (1993, 1996) has conducted a careful examination of these materials. Building on the work of Passas (1996), a reexamination of all these materials to provide a precise description of the evolution of the bank could help develop hypotheses about transnational organized crime or at least some major elements of it. Interviews with decision makers may well be an important component of such work, as it was for Alison's classic study.

A critical research decision is whether the unit of analysis is the offense, the offender, or the enterprise. For measurement purposes, the offense is the more tractable unit. For purposes of theory and case study, it is the offender or enterprise. In criminology there has been a great deal of attention to the offender and some attention to coffending, which allows for a distinction between acts and offenders for purposes of enumeration. In transnational organized crime the enterprise is also important—whether it is large or small, durable or transient, motivated by greed or a cause, protected by corrupt relations or trying to operate through secrecy.

IMPLEMENTATION STRATEGY

Transnational organized crime presents a long-term research issue. At this point it is possible to map out only the beginnings of a research agenda. Moreover, despite the political urgency of the problem, research funds for crime generally are extremely scarce (Wilson, 1997), and transnational organized crime will have to compete with spousal abuse, the deterrent effects of imprisonment, and a dozen other important topics.

In the short run, it is important to use available opportunities, particularly as a new area of research does well to establish its bona fides early. The growing interest of the International Monetary Fund and the World Bank in corruption as a central problem of development and governance will probably generate some related research activities at two institutions with strong research traditions. The United Nations Office for Drug Control and Crime Prevention has established a modest research program in this area; although that should not drive the U.S. effort, its existence and form should not be ignored. In particular, the UN has selected three crime types for its efforts: drugs, people trafficking, and corruption. The president's speeches have also given considerable emphasis to these same offenses.

The research agenda sketched here starts early in the process of conceptual and descriptive development. To attract good scholars into the field will require that some of the initial investment go to conceptual efforts that will demonstrate that this is more than a project of enforcement agencies with little patience or taste for scholarly work. Attracting good scholars to the field also will require a considerable funding investment, so that a long-term, systematic, rigorous, and objective program, characterized by well-established peer review procedures, can be mounted.

References

Abt Associates
    1997 *A Plan for Estimating the Number of "Hardcore" Drug Users in the United States.* Cambridge, MA: Abt Associates.

Adler, P., and P. Adler
    1985 *Wheeling and Dealing: An Ethnography of an UpperLevel Drug Dealing and Smuggling Community.* New York: Columbia University Press.

Alison, G.
    1971 *The Essence of Decision: Explaining the Cuban Missile Crisis.* Boston: Little Brown.

Blum, H., and R. Todd, eds.
    1999 *How the FBI Broke the Mob.* New York: Pocket Books.

Bovenkirk, F.
    1998 Organized Crime and Ethnic Minorities: Is There a Link? Paper presented at International Scientific and Professional Advisory Council conference in Courmayer, Italy, September 25-27. Available: Criminological Institute Bonger, Utrecht, The Netherlands.

Bureau of the Census
    1993 *We the American...Hispanics.* Report of the Ethnic and Hispanic Statistics Branch. Washington, DC: U.S. Department of Commerce.

Caldwell, G., and S. Galster
    1997 Crime & Servitude: An Exposé of the Traffic in Russian Women for Prostitution. Preliminary report for presentation at the conference on Criminal Justice Issues in the International Exploitation of Women and Children, sponsored by the U.S. Department of State, the U.S. Department of Justice, and the Federal Judicial Center, April 7. Available electronically: HtmlResAnchor www.xxxadvocate.com/html/crime_and_servitude.html#p08 [March 1999].

Caulkins, J.
    1990 What is the average price of a drug? *Addiction* 89(7):815-819.

1995 *Developing Price Series for Cocaine.* Santa Monica, CA: RAND.
Caulkins, J., and P. Reuter
1998 What can we learn from drug prices? *Journal of Drug Issues* 28(3):593-612.
Chin, K.
1990 *Chinese Subculture and Criminality: Non-Traditional Crime Groups in America.* Westport, CT: Greenwood Press.
1996 *Chinatown Gangs: Extortion, Enterprise and Ethnicity.* New York: Oxford University Press.
1997 Safe house or hell house? Experiences of newly arrived undocumented Chinese. Pp. 169-195 in Paul J. Smith, ed., *Human Smuggling: Chinese Immigrant Trafficking and the Challenge to America's Immigration Tradition.* Washington, DC: Center for Strategic International Studies.
1998 Transnational Organized Crime Activities. Paper presented at International Scientific and Professional Advisory Council conference in Courmayer, Italy, September 25-27. Available: School of Criminal Justice, Rutgers University.
Clawson, P., and R. Lee
1996 *The Andean Cocaine Industry.* New York: St. Martin's Press.
Cornelius, W.
1989 Impact of the 1986 U.S. immigration law on emigration from rural Mexican sending communities. *Population and Development Research* 15(4):689-705.
Cressey, D.
1969 *Theft of the Nation.* New York: Harper and Row.
Curtis, R., and M. Svirdoff
1994 The social organization of street-level drug markets and its impact on the displacement effect. Pp. 155-171 in R.P. McNamara, ed., *Crime Displacement.* New York: Cummings and Hathaway.
Dertouzos, J., E. Larson, and P Ebener
1999 *The Economic Costs and Implication of High Technology Thefts.* Santa Monica, CA: RAND.
Dombrink, J., and H. Song
1992 Asian Racketeering in America: Emerging Groups, Organized Crimes, and Legal Control. Unpublished final report under research grant no. 88IJ-CX-0049. National Institute of Justice, U.S. Department of Justice.
Feige, E.
1996 Overseas holdings of U.S. currency and the underground economy. In Susan Pozo, ed., *Exploring the Underground Economy.* Kalamazoo, MI: Upjohn.
Fijnhaut, C., et al.
1997 *Organized Cime in the Netherlands.* The Hague: Kluwer Law International.
Financial Action Task Force
1996 *FATF-VII Report on Money Laundering Typologies.* Available electronically: HtmlResAnchor www.oecd.org/fatf/rep_typologies.htm [March 1999].
Financial Crimes Enforcement Network
1996a Enhanced scrutiny for transactions involving the Seychelles. FinCen Advisory 1(2). Washington, DC: U.S. Department of the Treasury. Available electronically: HtmlResAnchor http://www.ustreas.gov/fincen/pubs/html [March 1999].

    1996b Mexican bank drafts and factored third-party checks. FinCen Advisory 1(6). Washington, DC: U.S. Department of the Treasury. Available electronically: HtmlResAnchor http://www.ustreas.gov/fincen/pubs.html [March 1999].

    1996c The global fight against money laundering. FinCen Advisory. Washington, DC: U.S. Department of the Treasury. Available electronically: HtmlResAnchor http://www.ustreas.gov/fincen/pubs.html [March 1999].

    1999 Enhanced scrutiny for transactions involving Antiqua and Barbuda. FinCen Advisory (11). Washington, DC: U.S. Department of the Treasury. Available electronically: HtmlResAnchor http://www.ustreas.gov/fincen/pubs.html [March 1999].

Finckenauer, J., and E. Waring
    1998 *Soviet Émigré Organized Criminal Networks in the United States.* Washington, DC: U.S. Government Printing Office.

Gambetta, D.
    1993 *The Sicilian Mafia.* Cambridge, MA: Cambridge University Press.

Gregory, F.
    1995 Transnational crime and law enforcement cooperation: Problems and processes between east and west in Europe. *Transnational Organized Crime* 1(4):105-133.

Grossman, M., F. Chaloupka, and C. Brown, eds.
    in press The demand for cocaine by young adults: A rational addiction approach. *Journal of Health Economics.*

Haller, M.
    1977 Bootleggers and American gambling: 1920-1950. Appendix 1 in Commission on the Review of the National Policy Toward Gambling. *Gambling in America.* Washington, DC: Commission on the Review of the National Policy Toward Gambling.

    1991 *Life Under Bruno: The Economics of an Organized Crime Family.* Conschohocken: Pennsylvania Crime Commission.

    1994 The Bruno family of Philadelphia: Organized crime as a regulatory agency. In Robert Kelly, Ko-Lin Chin, and Rufus Schatzenberg, eds., *Handbook of Organized Crime in the United States.* Westport, CT: Greenwood Press.

Ianni, A.
    1972 *A Family Business.* New York: Russell Sage Foundation.

Immigration and Naturalization Service
    1997 *Statistical Yearbook of the Immigration and Naturalization Service, 1996.* Washington, DC: U.S. Government Printing Office.

    1999 *Legal Immigrants, Fiscal 1997. Annual Report.* Washington, DC: U.S. Department of Justice.

International Organization for Migration
    1997 Prostitution in Asia increasingly involves trafficking. *Trafficking in Migrants.* Quarterly Bulletin, June(15).

Jacobs, J., and C. Panterella
    1997 Organized crime. In Michael Tonry, ed. *The Handbook of Crime and Punishment.* Oxford, England: Oxford University Press.

Jacobs, J., C. Panterella, and J. Worthington
    1994 *Busting the Mob.* New York: New York University Press.

Karch, S.B.
   1998   *A Brief History of Cocaine.* San Francisco: CRC Press.
Kennedy, M., P. Reuter, and K.J. Riley
   1992   *A Simple Model of Cocaine Production.* Santa Monica, CA: RAND Corporation.
Klockars, C.
   197   *The Professional Fence.* London: Tavistock Publications.
Lake, A.
   1998   Laying the Foundations for a New American Century. Presented at the Fletcher School of Law and Diplomacy. Available electronically: HtmlResAnchor http://usis.kappa.ro/USIS/policy-statements-on-romania/1996/eur0425.txt [March 1999].
Levitt, S., and S. Venkatesh
   1998   An Economic Analysis of a Drug-Selling Gang's Finances. Working Paper #6592. National Bureau of Economic Research, Cambridge, MA.
Lupsha, P.A.
   1995   Transnational narco-corruption and narco investment: A focus on Mexico. *Transnational Organized Crime* 1(1):84-101.
Maltz, M.
   1994   Defining organized crime. In Robert J. Kelly, Ko-Lin Chin, and Rufus Schatzenberg, eds. *Handbook of Organized Crime in the United States.* Westport, CT: Greenwood Press.
Manning, W., et al.
   1991   *The Cost of Bad Health Habits.* Cambridge, MA: Harvard University Press.
Martin, R.A.
   1998   *The Italian American Working Group: Why It Worked.* U.S. Working Group on Organized Crime. Washington, DC: National Strategy Information Center.
Marx, G.
   1998   Across borders. In William F. McDonald, ed., *Crime and Law Enforcement in the Global Village.* Highland Heights, KY, and Cincinnati, OH: Academy of Criminal Justice Sciences and Anderson Publishing Company.
Mueller, G.O.W.
   1998   Transnational Crime: Definitions and Concepts. Paper presented at the International Scientific and Professional Advisory Council conference in Courmayer, Italy, September 25-27. Available: School of Criminal Justice, Rutgers University.
Nadelmann, E.
   1990   Global prohibition regimes. *International Organization* (44)4:479-556.
   1993   Harmonization of criminal justice systems. In Peter H. Smith, ed., *The Challenge of Integration: Europe and the Americas.* Miami, and New Brunswick, NJ: North-South Center and Transaction Publishers.
   1993a U.S. police activities in Europe. In Cyrille Fijnhaut, ed., *The Internationalization of Police Cooperation in Western Europe.* Boston: Kluwer Law and Taxation Publishers.
National Insurance Crime Bureau
   1999   The NICB Vehicle Theft Study. Available electronically: http://www.nicb.org/theftstudy.htm [March 1999].

Office of National Drug Control Policy
- 1995 *What America's Users Spend on Illicit Drugs, 1988-1993*. Washington, DC: U.S. Government Printing Office.
- 1997 *What America's Users Spend on Illicit Drugs, 1988-1995* Washington, DC: U.S. Government Printing Office.

Paoli, L.
- 1997 The Pledge to Secrecy: Culture, Structure and Action of Mafia Associations. Unpublished Ph.D. dissertation, European University Institute, Department of Political and Social Sciences, Florence, Italy.

Passas, N.
- 1993 Structural sources of international crime: Policy lessons from the BCCI affair. *Crime, Law, and Social Change* 20(4):293-305.
- 1996 The genesis of the BCCI scandal. *Journal of Law and Society* 23(1):57-72.
- 1998 Transnational Crime: The Interface Between Legal and Illegal Actors. Paper presented at the Workshop on Transnational Organized Crime, Committee on Law and Justice, National Research Council, June 17-18, Washington, DC. Available: Department of Criminal Justice, Temple University.

Raine, L.P., and F.J. Cilluffo
- 1994 *Global Organized Crime: The New Empire of Evil*. Washington, DC: Center for Strategic and International Studies.

Reuter, P.
- 1983 *Disorganized Crime: The Economics of the Visible Hand*. Cambridge, MA: MIT Press.
- 1992 After the borders are sealed: Can domestic sources substitute for imported drugs? Pp. 163-177 in Peter Smith, ed., *Drug Policy in the Americas*. Boulder, CO: Westview Press.
- 1998 Book review of World Drug Report. *Journal Policy Analysis and Management* 17(4):730-733.

Reuter, P., and J. Haaga
- 1989 *The Organization of High-Level Drug Markets: An Exploratory Study*. Santa Monica, CA: RAND Corporation.

Reuter, P., and M. Kleiman
- 1986 Risks and prices: An economic analysis of drug enforcement. Pp. 128-179 in N. Morris and M. Tonry, eds., *Crime and Justice: An Annual Review*. Chicago: University of Chicago Press.

Saffer, H., and F. Chaloupka
- 1995 The Demand for Illicit Drugs. Working Paper #5238. National Bureau of Economic Research, Cambridge, MA.

Schlegel, K.
- 1998 Transnational Crime: Implications for Local Law Enforcement. Paper presented at the Workshop on Transnational Organized Crime, Committee on Law and Justice, National Research Council, June 17-18, Washington, DC. Available: Department of Criminal Justice, Indiana University, Bloomington.

Shelley, L.
  1998 Transnational Crime in the United States: The Scope of the Problem. Paper presented at the Workshop on Transnational Organized Crime, Committee on Law and Justice, National Research Council, June 17-18, Washington, DC. Available: Transnational Crime and Corruption Center, American University.

Simeone, R., W. Rhodes, and D. Hunt
  1997 *A Plan for Estimating the Number of "Hardcore" Drug Users in the United States.* Cambridge, MA: Abt Associates.

Singer, A., and D.S. Massey
  1997 The Social Process of Undocumented Border Crossings. Paper presented at the meetings of the Latin American Studies Association, Guadalajara, Mexico. Available on microfiche: Bell and Howell Information and Learning, Ann Arbor, MI.

Sparrow, M.
  1999 *Fraud in the Health Care Industry: Assessing the State of the Art.* Research in Brief. Washington, DC: National Institute of Justice.

Sutherland, E.
  1937 *The Professional Thief.* Chicago: University of Chicago Press.

Tonry, M.
  1997 *Ethnicity, Crime and Immigration.* Chicago: University of Chicago Press.

United Nations
  1995 *Fourth United Nations Survey of Crime Trends and Operations of Criminal Justice Systems.* Vienna, Austria: United Nations.

United Nations Drug Control Program
  1997 *Global Drug Report.* New York: Oxford University Press.

U.S. Department of State
  1999 Trafficking in women and girls – An international human rights violation. Fact sheet released by the Senior Coordinator for International Women's Issues. March 10. Available electronically: HtmlResAnchor http://www.state.gov/www/global/women/fs_9803110_women_traffick.html [March 1999].

U.S. Senate
  1996 *Hearing Before the Committee on Governmental Affairs.* Subcommittee on Investigations. Washington, DC: U.S. Government Printing Office.

Weatherburn, D., and B. Lind
  1997 The impact of law enforcement activity on a heroin market. *Addiction* 92(5):557-569.

Williams, P.
  1996 Introduction: How serious a threat is Russian organized crime? *Transnational Organized Crime Special Issue* 2(2/3):1-27.
  1998 Organizing Transnational Crime: Networks, Markets and Hierarchies. Paper presented at the Workshop on Transnational Organized Crime, Committee on Law and Justice, National Research Council, June 17-18, Washington, DC. Available: Ridgeway Center, University of Pittsburgh.

Wilson, J.Q.
    1997 What, If Anything, Can the Federal Government Do About Crime? Presented at the Lecture 1, Perspectives on Crime and Justice: 1996-1997 Lecture Series. National Institute of Justice, U.S. Department of Justice, Washington, DC.

Winer, J.
    1997a Alien smuggling: Elements of the problem and the U.S. response. *Transnational Organized Crime* 3(1 Spring):50-58.
    1997b International Crime in the New Geopolitics: A Core Threat to Democracy. In William F. McDonald, ed., *Crime and Law Enforcement in the Global Village*. Highland Heights, KY, and Cincinnati, OH: Academy of Criminal Justice Sciences and Anderson Publishing Co.

Appendix
Workshop on Transnational Organized Crime
June 17-18, 1998

AGENDA

June 17	**Members' Room, National Academy of Sciences, 2101 Constitution Ave. N.W., Washington, DC**
8:30 am	Opening Remarks and Introductions (coffee, juice, and pastries available) *Peter Reuter, chair*
9:30 am	National Institute of Justice's Workshop Goals & Interests *Jeremy Travis, Director, NIJ; Sally Hillsman, Research Director, NIJ*
10:00 am	Break
10:15 am	Presentation: Definition of Transnational Organized Crime *Louise Shelley, author; Jim Finckenauer, discussant*
11:00 am	Open Discussion
12:00 pm	*Lunch:* Presentation: The Organization of Transnational Crime *Phil Williams, author; Elin Waring, discussant*

1:45 pm	Open discussion
2:45 pm	Break
3:00 pm	Focussed discussion: Problems in the Measurement of Transnational Crime *Discussion led by Peter Reuter*
4:30 pm	*Adjourn*
June 18	**Members' Room**
8:30 am	Presentation: The Interface Between Legal and Illegal Activities (coffee, juice, and pastries available) *Nikos Passas, author; Tom Naylor, discussant*
9:45 am	Open Discussion
10:45 am	Break
11:00 am	Presentation: Implications of Transnational Crime for Local Law Enforcement *Kip Schlegel, author; Dan Schneider, discussant*
11:45 am	Open Discussion
12:30 pm	*Lunch:* Open Discussion of All Workshop Presentations
3:00 pm	Discussion of Research Needs; Plans for Workshop Publication